The Hate Factory
Teaching Children to Hate

Erica Carle

authorHOUSE®

AuthorHouse™
1663 Liberty Drive
Bloomington, IN 47403
www.authorhouse.com
Phone: 833-262-8899

Published by AuthorHouse 09/17/2020

ISBN: 978-1-4343-8549-9 (sc)

Print information available on the last page.

This book is printed on acid-free paper.

Foreword

What damage has been done! We are now realizing it on the grandest scale and scene. Upon every senseless and abhorrent act committed by young people to themselves and others, we shake our heads, murmur our prayers and wonder about what could have driven young minds to become so perverse and hopeless.

Nearly forty years ago a very prescient lady, Erica Carle, penned <u>The Hate Factory</u>, an early warning on the damaging effects of sociology in the classroom. Sociology and its Religion of Humanity replaced the truth of a God centered, created existence with man and earth centered worship.

Unlike the 'looking forward' view that Mrs. Carle had to take in the early 1970's, we now have the grim advantage of 'looking backward' on the carnage of lives and families resulting from the religion of sociology. It has been societal damage of epic proportions.

Sociology gained acceptance by having the audacity not only to call itself a science, but the mother of all sciences. Lacking any basis in scientific method, it includes so many variables any scientist would cringe at the prospect of deriving firm conclusions. Yet, at its very origin, this sociological point of view proudly declared itself the highest of scientific endeavors.

We were designed to appeal to and reach out to a higher power, not delude ourselves into thinking we are that higher power. When we believe that this higher power lies in this world, or even in us; what else can this breed but hopelessness and despair? God's Word tells us worship of things earthly, human or manmade is delusion and ultimately leads to our destruction. Daily experience confirms it.

Gradually and steadily over the past forty years, a sad and discouraging trend has continued to grow. The violence in our society, which once was insulated from and rarely initiated by our younger members, has exploded in frequency and savageness. In recent years campus shootings and random killings have gone to a dreadful new level, and no end is in sight. In almost all cases sociology and its humanistic tenets have destroyed the hopes and spirit of more than two generations of young.

During the past fifty years, nothing about our public education system is better. World rankings now find our students consistently falling out of even the top 20. Imagine that, number one to also-ran in two generations.

The Hate Factory is being published again in its original form. Included are the original comments and forewords of the day. The words in this small book of nearly forty years ago were sadly prophetical. Can we use them today, with the history of their foresight and intelligence in our rear view mirror? I believe we can, and that is why I urge you to carefully study and consider this book both in terms of the time in which it was written, and the events that have come to pass since that day.

Thanks for your wisdom and foresight Mom!
Your loving son, Eric John Peter

Foreword

By John Steinbacher

"If the changes were carefully engineered and not pushed too fast, Christians would not miss their Christ. People would no longer suffer the yearning for a God who loved them as individuals."

This is the theme of Erica Carle's masterful dissection of the direction of American education over the past several decades – a story of the betrayal of a whole school system and of the students who are "prisoners" within its walls.

Few Americans know the role played by sociologists in subverting the intellectual and moral capabilities of American schoolchildren. Even fewer know the relationship between the sociologists and what is happening, today, in the "great" Christian sects.

"In reality, sociology is not a science, not a search for objective truth, but a way of looking at life," writes the author of this book. "It is closer to a religion than a science, but it is destructive, not constructive. It is a religion of half truths, distortion, immorality and deception – a religion which does not seek truth but attempts to manufacture it. It is a religion which seeks to destroy, rather than perfect human nature and individuality. It has brought out the worst, rather than the best, in many of the young people who have been exposed to its teachings."

Over the years the sociologists – working hand in glove with social workers, psychologists, politicians and people of varied professional stripes – have set about to create a whole new world in their own distorted image, gazing at the world through a mirror, darkly, and never coming to a knowledge of the truth.

But it doesn't matter if the prime manipulators in this subversive war are trying to be Truth Seekers, or not. They are riding high on the crest of a wave that is crashing against all the familiar landmarks, dashing all before it in one confused, tumbled, chaotic mass of wreckage. It is Christian civilization that could ultimately be buried in that wreckage.

For the past five years this writer has warned that the number one battleground in America is the public school system. All too frequently our warnings have fallen on deaf ears. Christian people, who should have known better, have frequently been the staunchest supporters of the public school system which has been busily chipping away at all the Christian verities for the past five generations.

The public school system, for all too many Americans, has become their church, their religion, their holy of holies, their sanctum sanctorum. Blindly and unthinkingly they give allegiance to that which no longer merits their allegiance, even when they see the end product, their children, subverted and "changed" before their eyes.

This is not to say that all the teachers in the system are to blame. They are as much victims as are the children and the taxpayers – and many teachers are beginning to awaken, albeit rather late to do much about the situation.

But all is not lost. There is a shaking and a stirring in the land among those who are most able to make the changes necessary to save the system – the teachers and the parents. This shaking takes many forms – from confrontations before school boards to close monitoring of text books and audio visual aides – and all too often the forces of Right are routed by the overwhelming power of the combined forces of the Media and the professional educationists.

Still, enough local battles are being won, by enough people, to rattle the eyeteeth of the totalitarians. The sex education battle in Anaheim, California is one such example. (See the book, *The Child Seducers*). There are many, many others – battles fought by little known people who have no power, no "name," no degrees, no great wealth or influence. All they have is Truth on their side.

I have seen these people all over this great land, from Denver to New York City, from Kennewick to Charleston. Generally they are women, battling a system that frequently seems immovable and overwhelming, but fighting, nonetheless, with everything they have.

This is an exciting war, because the stakes are so high and the battle lines are so clearly drawn. The forces are in the field, and the first scattered shots have been fired. Americans must decide which army they will join in the days immediately ahead, because in this war there can be no neutrals, no conscientious objectors.

Some of us, by accident of history or by experience, have unwillingly been given the rank of generals in this war – but without all those thousands of privates and corporals on the front lines the officer corps would be surrounded and destroyed in short order.

We say it is an exciting war, but we also should add that it is often unpleasant and acrimonious, it is often downright messy, because those in power are not about to relinquish one iota of that power without a fearful struggle – and all too often they are in control of the principle bases of supply and communication and they have the vast army of tax supported "civil servants" to use as cannon foder.

When the war first began the attackers had little in the way of supplies and equipment and even less of communication through the Media. But that is beginning to change. No longer do the parents have to rely on guerilla tactics. Now the attack is frontal and major, on all sides, and in school district after school district the skirmishes have become fire fights in an effort to take the high ground.

Educator Publications came along at the just the right time in order to provide the supplies necessary for this basic ideological clash. Prior to the formation of this company there was no organization in the nation devoted to the battle over education. Now, thanks to all those foot soldiers out there, the books continue to roll off the presses in ever increasing numbers and the National Educator – the only paper in the country devoted to the parent side of education – continues to grow in subscriptions and in influence.

But all this is only a small part of what needs to be done if the public school system – and the private systems – are to be saved from those who would use them to destroy the American Dream.

Principally, the people of America must increasingly assume the responsibility for their own fate, as individuals who still have that right and that obligation in this free society.

In other words, Educator Publications will provide the tools of war, but the rank and file must seize those weapons by the millions and use them on the enemy if this war is to be brought to a just conclusion.

Over a hundred years ago, Cardinal Newman penned the immortal lines to a great hymn. Those words apply in today's world, as well, for they are timeless words for all generations.

"Lead kindly light, amidst the encircling gloom, lead Thou me on; the night is dark, and I am far from home, lead Thou me on. Lead Thou my feet, I do not ask to see the distant scenes – ONE STEP IS ENOUGH FOR ME."

Remember that – when all seems darkest. Take the high ground, one step at a time, and the battle will finally be won for you, for your children and for your beloved land.

(John Steinbacher is the managing editor of the National Educator and author of BITTER HARVEST: THE CHILD SEDUCERS and THE CONSPIRATORS: Men Against God, all available from Educator Publications). **NOTE: Now at Amazon.com**

Foreword

"Where did we go wrong?" Parents everywhere are asking themselves the same question. They have tried. They have wanted their children to be kind, happy, moral and productive adults, but so many parents have failed. Their children are bitter, filled with hate, resentment and disillusion – an easy mark for corrupters of all kinds. Their children no longer love them, respect them, or even listen to them when they speak. What has happened? Where **did** these parents go wrong?

This is a book for parents who blame themselves for the misery and distress of their children, and yet still can't discover what could have been done to make things different.

This is also a book for parents who have loving children and want to prevent them from joining the bitter, hate-filled, resentful and disillusioned millions.

This is a book for students. It is a book for students who have watched their friends change before their eyes – who have heard their friends pour out bitterness – who have seen them fall prey to corrupters, seducers, radicals and revolutionaries.

This is also a book for students who **hate**, but can't quite remember where or when they first began to **hate**. It is a book for students who are confused – who have heard one thing at home and another at school, at church, or from their friends.

This is a book for people, whether parents or not, who are puzzled by the moral, intellectual, and social degradation that have taken over so rapidly in recent years.

This is a book for teachers who have a sincere regard for and interest in their students; but who are being forced and pushed into changing their proven and effective methods to adopt unproven and puzzling experimental techniques. It is a book for teachers who have been wondering why textbooks are so changed and so devoid of real factual information.

This is a book for scientifically-minded who know there is no effect without a cause, and who want to know the cause of what is sometimes called 'the generation gap'.

THIS IS A BOOK FOR ALL WHO WANT ANSWERS, AND NOT CLICHES.

Introduction

The Threat

Any parent who has raised a family or who is pretty well along the way knows his children don't love him all the time. Even respect is given on a great deal less than 100 percent basis. There is no absolute perfection. There may even be bad moments when the only thing that holds a child to his parents is his dependence on them. But basic love, respect and family loyalty usually have been strong enough to carry most people over the times of turmoil, hard training, and disagreement. Under ordinary circumstances parents can sometimes be wrong, too harsh, even unworthy of respect, and still raise fine children who are kind and loving; and who lead happy and productive lives.

Years ago my father, who was a family physician, mentioned to me how remarkable it seemed to him that so often fine, intelligent, ambitious and loving children could be found in families of drunken, shiftless and even immoral parents. Doesn't it seem remarkable to you today that so many unhappy, disloyal, drunken, drug-crazed, shiftless, disillusioned and immoral children are found, not only in worthless families, but in families of fine, intelligent, productive and loving parents? Average parents, if they make an honest effort, should be able to raise children they can be proud of. Yet, today, even good parents are frequently failing. Why?

I would like to suggest to you that there is a cause for this unhappy reversal – for the increasing corruption and disillusionment of children – not a vague, generalized cause which 'society' must eradicate before you personally can begin to counteract it, but an active, persuasive force which each family can pinpoint directly to warn their children away from danger and protect them from it. Parents can minimize the effects of this pernicious influence if they know of its existence, how the persuaders reach their children, and what they are trying to accomplish.

Imagine someone going into your children's school or coming into your home who does his best to demoralize your children by dampening their enthusiasm for life and respect for themselves, degrading you and any moral principles you have taught them, and attempting to alienate them from you so future guidance and admonitions will have little effect. Wouldn't you wonder what his reason might be for such an audacious intrusion? What if he fills your children's minds with half-truths to mislead them, then deceives them into trying to bear intolerable burdens? Wouldn't you suspect he might be trying to use your children for his own purposes? Wouldn't you make an honest effort to discover just what he has in mind?

If you have been doing your human best to prepare your children for happy, productive, responsible lives; and he is breaking down the character you have been building, would you believe he could have their best interests at heart? If he tells your children things which fill them with doubt, despair, and ideas of destruction, larceny and hate, could you ignore him? Or would you, despite any mistakes you may think you have made in the past with your children, rally to their defense and protect them from an influence which could possibly ruin their lives, paralyze their intelligence, destroy their ambition, and rob them of any capacity for warmth and love?

The influence *is* there – working on your children, and not only on yours, but on the children of your friends, neighbors, relatives, and millions of other people who are strangers to you. These children are being deceived, 'treated,' and manipulated for a purpose. Not all of them will be destroyed, but many young people will be permanently damaged, and a great many more temporarily impaired.

Unless you have already had puzzling problems with your own children, or noticed undesirable changes in character and personality, you may be reluctant to believe there is a strong, highly-organized negative influence actively at work on young minds. You may not want to believe what I am going to tell you about the influence of the hate factories on children, but it will not be difficult for you to check. Once you have read the entire indictment, the evidence is as available to you as it is to me. The only way you can shut out the truth is by refusing to see it.

Unless your reactions are a great deal different from mine, you will be shocked, dismayed, angered and overwhelmed; but don't allow these emotions to paralyze your initiative. The stakes are high. The very lives and happiness of your own children are in jeopardy. The persuaders in the hate factories may be the most serious threat you will ever face in opposition to your efforts to raise fine, honest, well-balanced, productive and happy children, particularly if those children are just entering their teen years. Don't under-rate or ignore the threat.

Young people are being corrupted, discouraged, deflated, frustrated, over-burdened, and deceived. If you are a parent you need to find out who is trying to alienate your children's affection and persuade them to abandon the principles you have taught them. You need to find out who is teaching the young to hate family loyalty, Christian morality and Christian individuals, hate honest scientific investigation, hate independence, self-responsibility and achievement. You need to know so you will be able to take protective measures.

Let us go to the place where the persuaders do much of their work. Let us go with the children to the hate factory – to their sociology classroom.

While you may not be able literally to accompany your children to sociology class (although it would be a good idea to do so) you should be able without too much trouble to obtain a copy of the sociology textbook used in your school. It is probably available in the school library or high school bookstore. To gather material for this book I purchased copies of all the sociology textbooks used in my own area and experienced no difficulty.

It was no accident that I suspected sociology of a major role in child corruption. My study over the past ten years of the intent and history of sociology led me to surmise that sociology would most probably be playing a dominant role in forming the present day mental and emotional attitudes among young people, which in too many cases leads to erratic and destructive behavior.

I hope you will find a modern high school sociology textbook and go over it as thoroughly and critically as your time permits. You don't have to be a Ph.D. or even a high school graduate to learn enough to help your children, but you should be a thorough, careful and very attentive reader.

The Goal

I have been reading sociology books for quite some time, including some written more than a century ago, not because it is the world's most exciting diversion – you'll never believe how far that is from the truth until you read a few yourself – but because I have been looking for the pattern, checking to see whether sociologists throughout the history of the subject have been consistent in their beliefs, goals, and methods. They have!

While many of the books are deadly-dull, there is a fascination to the reading. The fascination is similar to that I once experienced watching a reformed pickpocket put on a demonstration of his 'art.' He performed his work with such finesse, such charm, and such apparent interest in and concern for his victims that the 'guinea pigs' who went up to the stage to help him in the demonstration never knew their pockets had been picked. They were positive he had been unable to fleece them, that the other participants were the victims, until the pickpocket produced watches, rings, billfolds, bracelets and earrings and laid them right on the table before them. He succeeded in stealing from them while they stood smilingly confident that he would not.

Why would anyone want to steal away love? Why would anyone want to alienate a child from his parents, tear down ambitions, zest for life and the principles on which a happy, independent, and productive life can be built? He would have to have an insidious and evil purpose.

Sociology has such a purpose. For nearly a century and one-half sociologically-oriented individuals have been making steady progress toward its accomplishment. When I tell that purpose to you, please do not say it cannot be true until you personally have checked the evidence. Sociology's stated ambition and goal is to take over the minds of succeeding generations of children in order eventually to rule the world and all its people – to fleece us, and all future generations out of our individual freedom. They have used sympathy, charm, deceit, distortion, outright lies and coercion. Yet, to a surprising degree, considering the damage they have done, they have escaped detection. Let us try to learn their thoughts, reveal their purpose, discover their methods, and understand why the children are their primary target.

Chapter 1

The Past

"Oh, you blind leaders who seek to convert the world by laboured disputations! Step out of the way or the world must fling you aside. Give us the Young. Give us the Young and we will create a new mind and a new earth in a single generation."
Benjamin Kidd[1]

The Lust

Ideas of world domination are not new. It has always been a favorite pastime of brainy individuals who have no taste for physical labor, trade, natural science or mechanical innovation to play the game of human engineering: speculating on and experimenting with methods of ordering and controlling other human beings. From the Greek philosopher, Plato, who compiled the ground rules, and gave many helpful hints, through all the lesser lights, up to and including our 20th Century fireflys, the 'noble' goal has been the same: a perfectly-ordered, eternally obedient 'society.' Only the name and characters have changed with sociology. The lust is the same, and Power is the name of the game.

What kind of mind could conceive and try to carry out an ambition to rule the world? What emotional twist would cause one to want to be among those who help fulfill that ambition? It is almost impossible for one who does not possess this type of mind to understand such

1

thinking. Don't allow the fact that you do not possess it lead you to deny its existence. Such minds *do* exist. They are already destroying, seducing or controlling many of the present generation of young people. The best description I have read of the emotional perspective of those possessed of this type of mentality was written by Edward Bellamy, a sociologically-oriented 19th Century writer. He said:

> "There is a lust of soul for soul dwarfing the lust of body for body, as the universal dwarfs the individual; a lust insatiable, a passion hopeless yet entrancing, sweeter in desire than all others in consummation."[2]

There are men who lust for other men's souls!

Sociological Builders

It is difficult to understand, but perhaps the sociological powerlust is a result of inflated ego combined with a warped sense of order.

Each of us has a sense of order and a necessity for order. We try to arrange our lives and our environment to conform to our individual requirements. While manner of expression and degree differ, the necessity for order exists in all of us. For example, a child when presented a box of blocks of varying sizes, shapes, and colors can't resist the urge to form those blocks into some orderly pattern or combination. Few people are comfortable if they notice a picture on the wall is wildly askew.

Much of the training we give our children is aimed at building on and improving their sense of order. Our language, music, art, and ability to count and calculate are all dependent on the fact that we can order and organize our thinking. Careful observation shows that our sense of order and harmony is but a minute expression of the order and harmony already present in nature and throughout the universe.

We each attempt to order our lives according to our own priorities. There are individual differences – most of them can be easily resolved; but people's goals do sometimes conflict drastically. Under the best of circumstances it takes great wisdom and a strong sense of individual justice for lawmakers to establish acceptable rules which do not conflict with nature or inhibit constructive activities.

When a brilliant dominating person with excess self-esteem interferes he can distort the entire picture and change intermittent conflict into chaos. Having no desire to satisfy his ego by his own talent, he sometimes chooses what to him is the greatest raw material of all for his 'genius' to cultivate and control: - other people. Instead of building in the material world with wood, steel and stone; or demonstrating personal skill; he trespasses, and constructs his monument to order out of human lives.

Because of the great variety of types of individuals and activities he fails to perceive natural order. He looks upon nature's infinite variety as chaos which he must put in order. His life is devoted to finding ways to overpower other minds – to cut off their thinking so his can be the factor which controls many lives. He assigns others their places and sees that they keep to them, organizing force to intimidate them where necessary. He does not see himself as wicked. In his own eyes he is a great benefactor for allowing lesser individuals to be ruled by his 'superior mentality':

> *"It is indeed an ambitious conception, this idea of blueprinting the outlines of a truly worthful society for the future and then politicing social evolution deliberately and intelligently toward that goal. There are those who regard such an ambition as ludicrously impossible. Yet this is the supreme aspiration of social science."*[3]

The Slave Mentality

None of us in our youth expect to be deceived by our teachers. We have faith in them and our parents. We are not, and we should not have to be, alert to detect intentional deception. Yet today's young people of high school and college age are members of the sixth generation who have been subjected to intentional deceit. We of the fourth and fifth generations have lost much of the truth ourselves, and as a result are often as bewildered as our sixth generation children.

A little history of thought is necessary to understand what has happened to our thinking in the past 150 years. The concept involved is one which has been argued since 500 B.C. and before. It is the concept of the 'one' versus the 'many'; of collectivism versus individualism; the state versus individuals. From a collectivist's point of view the necessary basic reality is the state. Individuals are but 'members' of the state.

Plato in his famous *REPUBLIC* wrote as a collectivist. He viewed the state as one large body, individuals existing only to serve the body. This point of view inevitably leads to slavery and violence because collectivists are forever trying to subdue individual minds and individual action which they believe will harm the unity of the state. Individuals have to be trained, not to promote their own happiness and worthwhile achievement, but to serve the needs of the state whatever the leaders of the state determine those needs to be. The collectivist's point of view is basic and necessary to tyranny.

On the other hand, according to the individualistic view, the state is merely a tool used by cooperating individuals to accomplish mutual goals. The state is created by, and responsible to, individuals. It is not a God to be worshipped, but a tool to be used with justice and discretion.

Once the necessity to tyranny of the collective concept is grasped it is easy to understand why Jesus was considered such a dangerous influence by representatives of the state. It was not that he stirred up terrible insurrections, not that he engaged in active political agitation, not that he desired control for himself, it was because he gave people knowledge of their individual importance to God. Each Christian said to himself, "I am an individual, God-created and important. I am individually responsible for my own actions. My salvation is individual. I am more than a mere member of a huge body called the 'State.' I am an individual serving Truth, and my God is Truth. I will have no more individuals being sacrificed. Don't tell me to place my children on the altar to appease the gods of the tribe or the state. Christ ended the necessity of human sacrifice. I am reconciled to my God through Him. Don't try to control me through collective guilt. My sins are individual, and through Christ my sins are forgiven."

Not all followers of Christ through the centuries understood their freedom or the full value of it. Many were blind worshippers. There were collectivists, however, who understood very well the danger Christianity posed to their ambitions. Some fought Christianity, others tried to adapt it and use it for their worldly purposes.

Many times throughout history the collectivist dogma has subdued entire populations and all but eliminated individual thought and action. However, in the late 18th and early 19th Centuries individual freedom was the dominant trend in the Western world: restraints on knowledge were going; new inventions and discoveries were making life fuller and more comfortable; America was offering unlimited opportunities to the courageous, ambitious, and enterprising; trade and travel barriers were falling, enabling individuals to seek the best of many lands; want and hunger were retreating; much was being done to alleviate human misery; science was gaining greater respect as the gifts won by careful observation and investigation were presented to the world. The trend seemed to be toward ever greater freedom, knowledge, and material abundance. People expected to rise or fall as a result of their own ability, industry, and good fortune. They no longer refrained from seeking their own answers to questions of the world around them. They no longer submitted to temporal power at variance with Christian conscience. Individuals were becoming ever more prosperous, ever more responsible. Thousands of educational institutions were being formed. Millions throughout the world were being schooled through the efforts of parents, churches, and voluntary groups. The children grew up in freedom under no obligation to state or ruler for their education.

To collectivists this was chaos. They hated individual thought and individuals who claimed sovereignty over their own minds. They saw the world, not as a world full of promise, challenges, and opportunities for growth and development, but as a world which frightened and dismayed them. There was no master plan, no individual or group of individuals taking charge of the lives of the masses. They yearned for a return to the slave mentality. While most were willing to admit that people prospered greatly with the increase of individual freedom, the collectivists could not conceive of living which left so many decisions to the individuals directly affected.

They got out their *PLATO* and began to bring his schemes for controlling people up-to-date. There were many ideas and many thinkers. However, as far as putting the collective ideas in a form which was suited to the time and emotionally satisfying to great numbers of people, one man stands so far above all the rest that understanding his goals and techniques for achieving them, and following the influence of his thinking on succeeding generations can give greater understanding of all the earlier, later, lesser, and auxiliary plans and planners. Most collectivist planners for the past century and one half have been either directly or indirectly influenced by his thinking.

The New Master Planner

Let us place the beginning in the year 1820. Our master planner was twenty two years old at that time, and he had already set his goal. He wanted nothing less than to reconstruct the entire religious, moral, scientific and political structure of the world. He believed his goal to be so worthy he dedicated his entire adult intellectual life to outlining his plan. His name was not God. It was Auguste Comte.

Comte was a patient master planner. He realized, above all, that before free people could again be brought under control their minds had to be trained to be willing to comply. He realized also, as Plato had, that such training could not be accomplished in one or two generations. He knew that a long range plan was necessary so each new generation could be trained to accept the loss of freedom and knowledge of the preceeding generation as the normal state of affairs. Many of us who are now so concerned about the trend in our country and the world are children of the fourth and fifth generations under his influence. Young people in high school and college are children of the sixth generation. Because it has been so long, all of us have been influenced by Comte's thinking in more ways than we can possibly realize or enumerate. Perhaps if properly informed the children of the sixth generation can begin to gain release from over 150 years of his ever hardening grip.

Comte's writings never were and never will be best sellers. He didn't want a large audience. He wrote for the intellectual elite of collectivism. He expected his ideas to be adapted by them to be given to future generations of collectivist intellectuals and through them to the young of future generations.

Comte's master plan had two vital branches. First, he turned his attention to science so his disciples and intellectual heirs could eventually claim precedence over all the sciences and guide all further development. His early writings were an attempt to bring all scientific investigation into an orderly controllable system. He praised the sciences and arranged them according to his conception of their importance and relative development; scientific advancement being regarded by him as a matter of evolution. Those sciences which had early beginnings, he stated, were in the final stages of evolution. their findings were governed by laws and could be considered positive knowledge. Other sciences were just coming of age, and were ripe for greater development. Above all the sciences Comte placed his new science, social science or sociology, the science of Society, highest in the hierarchy, ruler of all the sciences!

Comte based his new science on the idea of social evolution. He explained progress in terms of increasing collectivization. Beginning with individuals or small families wandering alone, humans were said to have progressed to larger and larger social groups. The final sought-after result will be when all are united into one great, well-disciplined body. The process of social evolution brings us ever closer to this goal, and it is the duty of sociologists to do everything in their power to speed the day of realization: to study and accelerate the social evolution of "Humanity."

As the theory of natural evolution gained greater acceptance, Comte's theory of social evolution attracted adherents among the uncritical; and on the basis of this theory, or as he regarded it, law of social evolution, sociology was accepted by many as a legitimate science. Proponents failed to note, however, that sociology differed from the physical sciences. Physical sciences depend above all upon observation, then collection of many observations, followed by comparison, arrangement and classification. All observations, however minute, are considered before forming an hypothesis. When conclusions are drawn from known facts, the scientific mind remains open to correction as future knowledge presents a wider view of the subject.

Sociology began, not by studying individuals and the differences between them, not by collecting actual observations, but with the conclusion itself: that all significant differences interfering with sociological control of 'Humanity' would eventually be eliminated. It demands belief that 'society' is evolving from the 'many' to the 'one' – that individual family relationships are but the training school for larger loyalties which will eventually replace them. Sociology is the 'science' by which this supposed evolution from individuality is to be intelligently controlled and advanced.

To bring sociology into the family of natural sciences, Comte merely redefined the world 'science' in his own fashion. Science, to Comteists, meant the pursuit of generalities. Sociologically speaking, scientists are those who pursue generalities. Comte, himself, believed facts not in agreement with his own general doctrine should be discarded:

> "In our search for the laws of society, we shall find
> that the exceptional events and minute details must be
> discarded as essentially insignificant, while science lays
> hold of the most general phenomena which everybody
> is familiar with as constituting the basis of ordinary
> social life."[4]

In unscientific fashion Comte sought not the truth of the senses, but a meeting of minds:

> "The requisite convergence of the best minds cannot be
> obtained without voluntary renunciation on the part of
> most of them, of their sovereign right to free inquiry."[5]

So you see, the founder of the world's newest 'science' was ready to abandon all search for truth if such truth interfered with his plan for control.

The Sociological Religion

Control of science and scientists was not enough. Individuals had to be controlled. A new religion was the door to many minds. In the early and mid nineteenth century it might have seemed as impossible to conquer Christianity as it would have seemed to take over and regiment science, but Auguste Comte was undaunted. Because he believed in no God, he did not hesitate to create his own. For God he substituted the idea of collective Humanity. Humanity itself was the Great Being which must be worshipped and served. Individuals were to be taught to sacrifice themselves for the sake of Humanity, to dedicate their lives to Humanity, to give up individual benefits if leaders told them they conflicted with what was the good of Humanity. When the Religion of Humanity was originated, a word was needed to express this concept which was then foreign to Western thinking, so Comte coined his own: 'altruism,' meaning otherism, and signifying individual abandonment to the collective whole.

Gradually Humanitarian altruism began to mean the same thing to many people as Christian charity. Didn't they both involve sharing? Humanitarian giving which had as its source self-abnegation and guilt for personal achievement came to be regarded as equal to, even better than, Christian charity which is inspired by self-respect and the desire to share good fortune with and elevate others.

Insofar as religious self-abnegation similar to that of Eastern religions was substituted for self-respect; collective divinity for individual integrity; and collective, unselective 'love' for devotion between individuals and families, the strength of Christianity as a force for developing self-respect, individual integrity, and personal independence was neutralized. This, of course, was Comte's goal, for then:

> "In the name of the past and of the future, the servants of humanity – both its philosophical and its practical servants come forward to claim as their due the general direction of this world. Their object is to constitute at length a real providence in all departments, - moral, intellectual, and material. Consequently they exclude once for all from political supremacy all the different servants of God – Catholic, Protestant, or Deist – as being at once behindhand, and a cause of disturbance."[6]

In his plans Comte divided people into two basic types: those who did not believe in God, and those who did believe. Those who did not believe in God, he decided, would become immediate followers of the Religion of Humanity. Those who did believe in God would be subjected to a long period of training and change. As generations passed both Christian and non-Christian religions could be brought closer and closer together until eventually all believers in God would be willing to become Catholic in a Catholic Church which had been taken over by Comte ideology. There would then be only Catholics and Humanitarians, and these two major religions, now almost alike, would eventually merge into one great world-wide, sociologically-controlled Religion of Humanity.

> *"When the religion of science is inaugurated...man will confide in the 'sociologians' just as during the palmist days of the Catholic Church he confided in theologians; with this great difference, that the disciples of the religion of science will be their own judges with respect to results, which are produced in this matter-of-fact world."*[7]

If the change were carefully engineered and not pushed too fast Christians would never miss their Christ. People would no longer suffer the yearning for a God who loved them as individuals; for a Holy Spirit, the Spirit of Truth to give their minds comfort, inspiration, and lead them to knowledge; for Jesus who promised forgiveness of even the most monstrous sins to free them from the slavery of guilt. Instead, 'Humanity' would provide love. 'Society' and sociologists would provide their comfort and direct their thoughts, and much of what used to be called personal guilt could be redeemed by paying the 'debt to society' – or forgotten because many sins would be attributed to faults of 'society.' There would be no need for personal forgiveness because there would be no personal guilt left to forgive.

The Plan Takes Hold

While most of Comte's mental energy was devoted to the drafting of his diabolical design for world domination; he knew, despite his feverish mental exertion, the day of realization would not be within his own lifetime. Rather than discourage his efforts, this fact has its own fascination. It gave him, he believed, a spiritual unity with the future.

During the first generation Comte's teachings were already exerting a strong influence on the thinking of scholars, certain ministers, political theorists, and even some politicians. The strongest influence was among collectivists who were ready for his new religion and science – those who shared his conviction that individual minds must be subdued and trained to fit the planned evolution of 'society,' and who were looking for a workable plan to gain control of people's minds.

Educationally progress of Comte's design to change and eventually eliminate Christianity and take control of science, religion and world politics proceeded from the top down. During the first and second generations his ideas were much discussed by philosophers and intellectuals. Some of those who were most impressed took active steps to disseminate them. By the third generation there was much talk of religious unity. A giant World Parliament of Religions was held at the Columbian Exposition in Chicago which promoted sociology and the idea of religious unity. It was attended by thousands of representatives of every faith from all over the world. Some colleges offered courses in sociology and political science.

Early in the fourth generation many more colleges opened departments of sociology, although they were not always accepted by other members of the academic community. By the end of the fourth generation the college coverage was nearly complete and the children were beginning to receive instruction in sociology in high schools.

By the fifth generation history, geography, economics and ethics had all but lost their separate identity in most elementary schools. They were considered under the blanket title, 'social studies.' This served to incorporate the prestige of all the separate fields of learning into the 'social studies' area, thus adding to the respectability of sociology or social 'science.'

Children of the sixth generation have had in their schooling a near-complete sociological education. Even such subjects as mathematics, English, and foreign languages are taught with sociological implications and for sociological purposes. There has been no escape from sociological indoctrination for members of the sixth generation. Christian or non-Christian – all have been directed toward the Religion of Humanity.

To realize how subtle the change which has brought us to this point has been, all you need is a dictionary. Look up the word 'humanitarian.' See if you do not find the same definition of Humanitarian which I find in mine.

My 1954 WEBSTER says:

> "The distinctive tenet denying the divinity of Christ; also the system of doctrine based on this view of Christ. 2. The doctrine that man's obligations are limited to and dependent alone on, man and human relations. B. The doctrine of Saint-Simon* that a man's nature is perfectible through his own efforts without divine grace. 3. Regard for the interests of mankind; benevolence."

Now I think, whether you are a Christian or not, you will agree that being a Christian should mean more than being a good person who is nice to other people. There were nice people long before Christianity. There are nice people today who are not Christian. I think you would acknowledge that to be a Christian in the true sense of the word one would have to believe that Christ was the Son of God, that He was crucified to end for all time the necessity of human sacrifice for sins either collective or individual, and that the Holy Spirit remains as a guide and comforter. Logically one cannot be a Christian and at the same time deny the divinity of Christ. If he denies the divinity of Christ, although he may be a nice person, he is not a Christian.

Now think back. Can you ever recall hearing a nominal Christian object to being called Humanitarian? Yet an Humanitarian is one who denies Christianity. A Christian cannot be an Humanitarian. If thinking in six generations has become so confused that even Christian ministers allow themselves to be called Humanitarians

---

* Saint-Simon was one of Auguste Comte's early teachers.

and are willing to study sociology as a required part of their training, Comte has indeed come a long way without making too many waves. When you find individuals claiming to be both Humanitarian and Christian; collectivist and individualist; against war and in favor of coercing everyone into a collectivist 'society'; scientifically-minded, yet blind to individual differences – you must know something serious has happened to their thought processes or their means of communication. They are not talking sense. If we of the fourth and fifth generation sometimes speak so carelessly, it is small wonder those of the sixth generation are sometimes confused.

Children of the Sixth Generation

It is the children of the sixth generation who have been the most grievously wounded. They get little recognition for personal achievement, for personal ambition, for personal virtue. The goals that are within their reach; to produce goods; to trade; to offer services to other individuals; to invent; to entertain; to discover, and profit personally from their own productive efforts – these goals have been degraded and made to appear boring by their sociological education.

The collectivist goals which are impossible, outside the realm of personal achievement, or only possible through coercion and violence are thrust upon them. Before they have had an opportunity to prove their own ability, show their own worth or earn their own money they are asked to sacrifice their lives to others, to sensitize themselves to all Humanity. They are told vaguely that they must work to 'improve society,' 'enforce equality,' 'equalize opportunity,' 'eliminate poverty,' 'serve Humanity.' The way to accomplish these ends is to engage in political coercion and submit to sociological direction. The children of the sixth generation are being trained to be blind to themselves, to their own individuality, to see themselves only as members of 'Humanity'; to accept 'Society' as their moral teacher. 'Society' as their critic. 'Society' as their disciplinarian. 'Society' as their God.

It is no accident that the sixth generation is becoming the generation of violence, of drugs, of promiscuity, of self-contempt. They have been taught that individuals are important only as members of 'society.' Some resent 'society' for denying them their individuality. They may do violent things to punish 'society'; behave promiscuously to show 'society' does not rule them; or cloud their minds with drugs. Others struggle to gain 'society's' approval by humanitarian dedication.

The only surprising and encouraging thing is that even after six generations there are still so many who retain their personal integrity. While they cannot help but be confused they are seeking something better for themselves than a drug-induced conformity, a life of protest, or a life of dedication to 'Humanity.' There are many of the sixth generation who want to learn Truth, to earn, to achieve, to produce, to help other people with their own effort and their own money; to keep their bodies and their minds clean, to love and be loved as individuals. There will be more young people of this type if we of the fourth and fifth generation, and those of the sixth generation who are able, can help lift the veil and return to true knowledge, to honest science which conforms to the evidence of our senses, to language which is precise and accurate as a means of honest communication, to history which is untainted by sociological interpretations, to an appreciation of individual differences and individual goals.

Chapter II

High School Sociology Today

"Everything depends upon passing out the expert opinions of the social scientists to the masses of the people; and the schools, particularly the high schools, are the only adequate agency available for this function."

A SCOCIOLOGICAL PHILOSOPHY OF EDUCAITON, P. 242
Ross L. Finney, Ph. D.
MacMillian Company, 1929

Training for Dependence

A parent casually picking up a high school sociology text might find some cause for resentment and alarm, but it would not be easy to discern the over-all pattern and direction of teaching without knowing in advance where the sociologists are headed.

It is no secret that they are driving for power. Many books can be found in which the intent is clearly stated, or in which the necessity for sociological direction of world affairs is assumed. After reading these books, particularly those written by early sociologists who were engaged in teacher training or theological instruction, it becomes easier to understand why so many sociological humanitarian efforts to improve living conditions fail or make things worse. Improvement of the human condition was never the true goal.

The true goal has always been to increase sociological power. The schools are used to prepare children for this increased sociological dependence. If their training is effective it will accomplish some of the following purposes:

1. To develop emotional rather than intellectual responses to what are called 'social problems.'
2. To direct emotions toward collective rather than individual or family relationships.
3. To train students toward self-sacrifice rather than self-respect.
4. To convince students that as individuals they are ineffective – that worthwhile goals must be pursued through group effort or under group control.
5. To idealize distant, long-range and even impossible achievements so people can be bound together in common effort for indefinite periods of time.
6. To alienate children from parental influence and Christian moral teaching.

The Mask

The first step in an elementary sociology text, as it is with any seducer, is to build up trust and confidence. Within the first few chapters most of them will attempt to convince their readers that sociology is a science. Few children will question the claim or attempt to look behind the mask. They do not expect to be deceived. Hardly knowing what is meant by science, they accept without thinking. Once they have accepted sociology's scientific mask they become less likely to question and more likely to accept its teachings as scientific truth.

In reality sociology is not a science, not a search for objective truth, but a way of looking at life. It is closer to a religion than a science, but it is a destructive, not a constructive religion. It is a religion of distortion, half-truth, immorality and deception – a religion which does not seek truth, but attempts to manufacture it. It is a religion which seeks to destroy, rather than perfect human nature and individuality. It has brought out the worst, rather than the best in many of the young people who have been exposed to its teachings.

Sociology or 'social science' is the religion which attempts to destroy individuals by denying their existence, by telling them they have no 'self' apart from social interaction. To a sociologist there is no such creature as an individual human being who uses his own intelligence and acts on his own initiative. We are all but members of a larger body who have no real existence outside that larger body. The intelligence of the larger body acts on us and controls us. We react and respond, but have no free will. Sociology's aim is to achieve a world which conforms to the mind-destroying ideals of the sociological religion.

> *"Physically we have become separate; mentally we remain but slightly differentiated participants in a common social plasm. Each person acquires a mind of his own only as he participates in the social mind. The notion of a separate and independent ego is an illusion."*[8]

Man and Social Change

I have a number of high school sociology books before me. If you will refer to yours, you will find they are all quite similar in many respects. All sociologists, for example, talk about 'social change.' The preface may begin by announcing that we live in an age of 'social change.' The statement seems so obvious to most people that it is hardly worth mentioning. Change is everywhere all the time. But note that the sociologist said 'social change.' There is a difference between what the sociologist means by 'social change,' and what an uninformed, casual reader might think he means. Unless we pin down and limit the meaning of the expression we lose the battle for our children before we begin to fight. 'Social change' is not a precise term unless its meaning is limited to changes in dealings between individuals and their relationships with one another, and changes in political demands and prohibitions. Do not include scientific advancement or technological progress in your understanding of this phrase. If you do, this allows the sociologists to gain your consent for their 'sociological change' on the basis of the fact you approve of greater knowledge and the cultural and material benefits which result from it. Because you accept changes in knowledge and the physical environment, sociologists use your acceptance as affirmation for the general idea of change – minimizing he possibility that you will question them when they begin to promote the 'social changes' which lead toward their goal of complete central control: collectivizing and centralizing authority, responsibility and power, leaving individuals without authority over their own lives – irresponsible and powerless.

> *"We can have an ideal society only when every person volunteers to sacrifice himself for the good of the whole."*[9]
> THE RECONSTRUCTION OF RELIGION P177
> Charles A. Ellwood, Ph.D.
> Professor of Sociology, U. of Missouri
> MacMillan Company, 1923

There is a sociological manner of speaking which should be understood. Sociologists talk about 'mankind' and 'man' and most high school sociology books will mention at least once that 'man' knows more about regulating nature than about controlling himself. They do not mean an individual man knows little about controlling himself (Although that is sometimes true), or that individual men know little about controlling themselves (also true on occasion); they are talking about group or political control. They are really saying that the few who aspire to unquestioned leadership have not yet achieved control over individual minds and actions.

> *"The purpose of studying sociology is that mankind may learn the rational control of social relations."*[10]
> OUR CHANGING SOCIAL ORDER P17
> Gavian, Gray & Groves
> D.C. Health & Company, Boston, 1941

Watch out when sociologists say 'mankind' or use the singular words such as 'man' in a plural sense. If you analyze the sociological use of singular nouns for plural realities, you will frequently find that it is done to obscure the fact that individual thoughts and individual actions are involved; but the sociologist does not want you to take note of the fact. They do not like to acknowledge the existence of individual intelligence.

Scientific Corruption

Truth should be our measure of merit. If sociologists were really scientists, if they spoke the truth without distortion, we could respect them. Because of their lies and attempts to deceive, we should dismiss them and their 'science.'

In the case of the particular book I am holding now, I don't have to go further than the first paragraph of the first chapter to find an example. Chapter one is the 'sell sociology as a science' chapter. One of the methods the sociologist uses to attempt to build his 'science' is to degrade the level of thinking and scientific intelligence of previous generations. The author announces that in Colonial times if a healthy man died in bed there was a 50-50 chance his widow would be tried for witchcraft. This is an outlandish distortion! Try to prove even one such case with the best historical evidence. After such a whopper he proceeds to tell students how in our enlightened age 'we' base our conclusions on study and evidence, not witchcraft.

Would your teen-aged children read carefully enough or have enough historical knowledge and interest to question a teacher on a seemingly inconsequential point? Perhaps it is unimportant in itself, but when there are many 'inconsequential' little slips of this type in high school sociology textbooks a student can be put in a state of utter confusion and complete exhaustion trying to maintain his intellectual integrity and respect for truth.

The scientific techniques on which sociology's claim to the name of 'science' is based include: questioning people, observing people, gathering statistics about people, and sometimes setting people up in a 'laboratory situation' so their reactions can be observed. This is called scientific investigation. The results of this gossip, spy, and 'what do people think?' kind of research are called scientific evidence. Sociologists' observations are supposed to be more valid than yours or mine because they count, tabulate and draw conclusions.

But sociology's credentials have been faulty from the start. Because the physical scientists in attempting to unravel nature's mysteries usually discover a pattern and organize their material to conform with nature's patterns, sociologists believe that if they organize they are scientists. They work from exactly the opposite direction. They build up the framework of organization, and then try to get nature to conform. They classify people and their associations and strain to fit individuals into one category or another – never seeing an individual human being with individual abilities, values, and goals. They cloud, rather than increase our ability to discover cause and effect relationships.

Techniques of the Unscience

Despite the fact that from its inception sociology has had goals which negate the possibility of honest conclusions from honest evidence, many people do pay heed to advice from sociologists – the most dangerous for your children being teachers and school administrators, and the most dangerous for individual liberty being sociologically trained and oriented politicians and governmentally financed social researchers.

As you read your sociology book keep asking yourself questions. While you can't dwell on each of the little inconsistencies, misstatements, contradictions, assumptions, devices, distortions and untruths, you will find; be alert so you are aware of them. For example: If the sociologist makes a statement such as 'A child at birth has no self and is not aware of himself as distinct from others,' ask yourself how he could possibly learn such a thing.

Watch for devious means to plant ideas. One book in the 'promote sociology as a science' chapter mentions a playground situation saying dominance among boys is achieved by threats and arguments, leaving one with the impression that childhood dominance is violently achieved. This half-truth serves more than one sociological purpose. First, it is an effective way of degrading voluntary childhood associations because it overlooks the positive fact that the dominant individual in a group of boys is not usually the bully, but more often the one who has a happy friendly personality and a head full of ideas for having fun. The negative sociological view can have an emotional effect on students. It may even give the unpopular high school student cause to look down on his popular fellow classmates – and perhaps start him on the self-destructive road toward hating successful people. In addition, if the student accepts the statement without question, it diminishes his ability to read critically and extract truth from his reading material.

> *"...If it were possible to control the learning of all individuals, in the way both of ideas and of emotional attitudes, as they come on to the stage of life, it would be possible to modify the whole complex of our social life, or our civilization, within the comparatively short space of one or two generations."*
> CHRISTIANITY AND SOCIAL SCIENCE P19
> Charles A. Ellwood
> MacMillan Company, 1923

Another technique I noticed in several books is that of using works of fiction as sociological evidence or to draw examples of undesirable behavior. This is done to promote some type of sociological legislation or to gain approval for sociological legislation of the past. However, consulting fiction is hardly an honest way for a true scientist to get his information about people.

Sociologists are also prone to invent hypothetical situations, then interpret them in such a way as to build up resentments and desired sociological attitudes in the students. One book discusses an exuberant youngster who was frequently in trouble because of his boyhood pranks. His young adult life was filled with practical jokes, misdemeanors, and unconventional actions. Finally he took a sales job and had great success – even worked up to a position of authority. He married and had a family, worked conscientiously and rejected all reminders of his past irresponsible behavior. You and I might say he had finished with his childish fun, and had learned to assume and enjoy his adult responsibilities. In the sociologist's view, which is the one your children learn, their hypothetical person had succumbed to the unrelenting pressures of social conformity. His case was presented as if, after years of discipline and repression, his spirit had finally been broken.

Sociologist writers sometimes assert that they as sociologists and 'scientists' are concerned with 'what is,' and not what 'ought to be.'

It is surprising how many of them in the very next chapter, or even the very next paragraph complain because there is great resistance to sociological or social change, and talk about sociological research and application of that research as an effective means for making over the world.

Since sociology is supposed to be the study of groups, and since the road to power is through the construction, use, consolidation and control of groups; sociologists attempt to bind students to the idea of groups. Instead of saying 'family,' they say 'primary group.' Instead of saying 'friends,' they say 'peer groups.' Instead of saying employers, associates, teachers, etc., they say either primary or secondary groups. Those who are outside are deviants or non-conformists.

Frequently sociologists have to strain to a ridiculous degree to fit people into group classifications. A pair of lovers constitute a sociological group. The whole female sex is called the 'female sub-culture.' Sociologists speak as if groups form individuals, when in fact individuals who have a common purpose form groups. But even people without a common purpose and no personal contact can be put in a sociological group – the 'out' group. A nasty child, if he becomes a real problem or delinquent is a member of the 'delinquent sub-culture' even if he has no association with other delinquents.

It is ridiculous how sociologists strain and push to create the impression of unity and scientific integrity. Yet, it is easy to be taken in if one is not 100% alert. The writers of the books are real professional con artists, and very patient and clever. If we were to use their means of classification, we might say they belong to the same sly, delinquent sub-culture as the professional pickpockets.

Heredity Environment and –

After the chapter on sociology as a science you will probably find some paragraphs, or more likely, a chapter or two on heredity vs environment. Sociologists have been going around in circles on this matter for almost as long as sociology has existed. Most of us would be willing to acknowledge that both heredity and environment are of great importance in forming the personality and character of an individual and determining his course in life. When physicians, geneticists, and psychologists appear with unquestionable proof that certain characteristics are more strongly dependent on one than on the other we are willing to listen and guide ourselves accordingly; but the endless discussion of heredity vs environment after the importance of both has been granted would seem to serve no purpose.

Don't be too sure!

The pickpocket distracts your attention by an obvious maneuver while by unnoticed subtle moves he steals away your valuables. While we are arguing for or against heredity and for or against environment and assigning importance and debating the contributions of both we tend to forget one equally important element in a person's makeup – his free will or his spirit – his own choice as to how he will use his gifts or overcome the obstacles heredity or environment have placed in his way.

The sociological argument of heredity vs environment distracts one from recognizing the existence of such a free will and puts human beings on an animal level as creatures who react and respond, who must be maneuvered into the 'proper' condition. It does not recognize them as thinking individuals capable of conceiving and perceiving intangible moral principles and directing their own lives.

The denial of moral principles and an individual's freedom to choose may be one reason many children fare so badly today. They are told they are under the power of groups – that morality is decreed by groups, - that their personality was formed by groups – that they are made to adhere to the standards of groups. It could make them feel helpless, caged in, pushed by 'Society.' They are left with only two choices: conform or rebel! Those who conform deny themselves and live for others, the group of Society. Those who rebel give up trying, or look for ways to destroy or break down the 'system.'

Life would be so much easier for them to comprehend, freer and more enjoyable if they were taught basic truths and principles rather than sociological obedience to the group. The young people who have the best chance to retain their identity and integrity are those who pay the least attention to or do not understand their sociological instruction, who somehow manage to escape indoctrination.

What a disaster, if the only students who can maintain their integrity are those who reject or ignore their training! At one time many children received good training outside the home. Even if a child had parents who were a poor example he learned in school and in church the basic principles to apply to his own life. He learned to evaluate individuals and not to conform to the group. He learned he did not have to be immoral, dishonest, lazy or disagreeable just because some others in his family or among his associates were. He was taught to be careful in choosing friends because bad behavior is easier to learn than good. He learned he could rise above his handicaps and surroundings. He learned that whatever his situation in life he could improve it by his own effort. He was free and he knew it! He was taught to take the blame for his mistakes and to accept without guilt the rewards of his virtues and good fortune. He had an incentive for hard work, an appreciation for the gifts he received and a spirit that gave him strength to fight against adversity and persist in the accomplishment of his goals.

He was not taught to shoulder the guilt for the misdeeds of his ancestors, although he knew he could learn from their mistakes. He learned that he, himself, not others, bore the largest share of responsibility for what he was to become. While he was urged to be charitable toward others he was not burdened with the fruits of their errors, immorality, and failures. What he did in his own life mattered. It made a difference. He was taught his character and achievements were important to himself and to God – and 'God' was not 'Society,' 'Humanity,' or the 'Group.' Material comforts for some may have been few. Work may have been difficult. Life may have been hard, but to the one who respected himself as an individual it was never futile or without meaning.

'Self' Destruction

Recently while visiting a young cousin in college my husband became involved in one of the rap sessions at the fraternity house. The subject of drugs was brought up. One young man listened for a while and then said, "I'll tell you one thing, LSD showed me who I really am."

"You stupid idiot!" my husband joked, "there never was a time when I didn't know who I was. If you're having such a hard time, bring me all your coats and shirts. I'll have little labels with your name sewn inside. Then every time you wonder who you are you can unbutton and take a look."

Everybody laughed, and the discussion continued. It wasn't until I began to read modern high school sociology books that the real tragedy of this little drama hit me with its full impact. The statement about LSD did not indicate a smart aleck trying to show off. It was not an affectation, nor was it a rationalization to justify stupid behavior. That poor boy actually did not know who he was. In his own eyes he had no real identity. He was literally trying to find his 'self' in drugs.

Hundreds of thousands of young people today are in more or less the same situation. Their problem is a great deal more serious than their parents realize, have ever experienced, or possibly could even understand. These lost souls are wandering around seeking, but never finding, that elusive something called 'self.' They seek it in their relationships with other people. They seek it in travel. They seek it in outlandish dress and hair styles. They seek it in sexual activity. They seek it in drugs or debauchery. They seek it in service and self-sacrifice. They seek it in crime – perhaps hoping that someone somewhere will make it clear to them who they really are.

How could it be? How could so many be similarly afflicted? Is there some common cause to which all of them have been exposed? How could anyone doubt his own identity? We all have minds. We have bodies. What is it we perceive when we look in the mirror? It is a reflection of something! Do we not see ourselves?

According to sociologists – No! The 'self' to a serious student of sociology is the opinion of other people – or what one imagines other people's opinion of him to be. A newly born child, according to sociological thinking has no 'self' because he has not interacted with the groups that make up his social environment. High school young people are told they were born without a 'self.' They have no identity, no soul. It must be given to them by 'Society.'

Do you know any high school aged individual intellectually equipped to battle that one out with the sociologists? They parrot the sociological phrases. Many of them believe. Why not? One does not expect to be deceived by his teachers. They believe, but they cannot accept. Without knowing where to look, which way to turn, or even what they are looking for, they begin the pitiful, heartbreaking search for identity. They have to find themselves and they don't know where to look.

What would you tell somebody who is actually looking for his 'self?' Where would you tell a youth to look for his own identity? How do you talk to a youth who believes he has no 'self?' Can you talk to him about self-respect? He has no self. Can you talk to him about self-confidence? He has no self. Can he have self-control? He has no self. Self-reliance? He has no self.

If your child contracted no other mind-corrupting concept from sociology, the loss of 'self' could be enough to destroy him. He can be blinded to his own individuality. He can find identity only as a member of a group.

The sociological child is born into a group – the family. He is molded by the group. There is nothing but groups. There is he kinship group, the religious group, the play group, the common interest group, the army group, the medical group, the 'in' group, the 'out' group – everything is groups. Any time he meets another person the sociology student is told he is interacting in a 'group situation.' A young person with such training loses his ability to recognize his own unique personality. If parents are not aware of how he is being trained they are not even alerted to the fact that he needs help. The sociologists can train him their way.

> "The young mind is as absorbent as blotting paper. The ideas of other people exert an insistent pressure even upon adults unless we are already possessed of ideas with which they seem to conflict. As a young child's mind is so meagerly equipped as yet with knowledge, it can offer no such resistance. Accordingly, it absorbs whatever cognitive material happens to be extant in its social environment."[12]

What about churches? Don't they help young people recognize their own value? Many do, of course. However, one of the major goals of Auguste Comte, the sociologists, and sociologically oriented people who followed Comte's intellectual pattern was to take over or destroy Christianity. Then as generations passed the Christian religion which spoke to and cared for individual souls could be replaced by the sociological religion which deals only with groups and social issues. Many priests and ministers today have been sociologically trained and no longer speak of individual identity, individual concern, individual guilt, and individual salvation. They preach on social issues, abhor talk of a personal relationship with God, and refuse to acknowledge individual souls. They augment rather than counteract the sociological destruction of 'self.'

> *"The nation is not a mass of independent individuals, but of related individuals, who, moreover are so closely related that they make together an indivisible organism; this organism develops according to orderly laws; this organism has perpetuity, never disjoining itself either from its past of future; and the organism has also self-consciousness and moral personality. This is the nation in which we live and move and have our being."*[13]

In some cases this may be due more to ignorance than malice. There are ministers and priests who have had ample training in sociology, but their knowledge of history, Latin, Greek, Hebrew, the natural sciences and the Bible frequently does not compare with that of an ordinary 19th century schoolboy. They are better trained in urban sociology than the New Testament.

A lost child looking for 'identity' does not need a lecture on self-sacrifice, the troubles of 'Humanity', and urban sociology. He needs to be told that he has a *self* – that whatever may happen to him, *he* is important, and his response to the challenges which are given him is important. He needs to be told the opinion of the world is not the directing force; but that he should be guided by Truth and personal integrity. He needs to be shown how to discover, use, and multiply his talents. He needs to be warned against trespassing and uninvited interference in the lives of others. He needs assurance that he is not bound by unbreakable chains to every other individual no matter how evil or depraved. He needs to be freed from the sociologist's destructive concept of the group as an organic entity.

The Narrow Room

No one can know exactly how another person feels, but when I see young people of the sociological generation (the generation that has had a complete sociological education), I wonder whether they might be experiencing the same trapped feeling I used to get from certain movies and in geography class.

If we kids didn't go to the movies on Saturday, we had to go on Sunday, because the hero of the adventure serial was suspended from a cliff or surrounded by Indians, about to be tortured by the mad scientist, or dropped into a vat of bubbling acid. We knew he would escape, but were quivering with anticipation to discover how. Sometimes the escapes were ingenious and exciting. Other times simple and obvious, but we never tired of the suspense.

Strangely, there was only one sequence which gave me bad dreams. In it the hero and his sweetheart had been deceived by a half-crazed inventor into entering a long narrow room. Within minutes they were horrified to discover that the walls were moving. Bit by bit, inch by inch, the walls were coming closer and closer together. I used to dream myself in that room with them. There were no doors and only one small circular window at the long end of the room through which we could see the wild-eyed inventor as he turned the crank bringing us closer and closer to our doom. I don't know how we escaped if we ever did. All I could remember were the walls moving slowly, relentlessly closer and closer. We couldn't help ourselves. I would wake up gasping for air and pushing against the wall.

Perhaps the comparison seems farfetched logically, but I used to get the same suffocating, hemmed-in emotion in geography class when we studied India. We learned how poor Indians were and how they suffered from famine and disease. It wasn't the poverty and illness which made me feel the walls were closing in. I was sure that if I were poor or sick I could do something to overcome my problems or find someone to help me. The oppressed squeezed-in feeling came from the fact that religious beliefs, customs and government restrictions tied men's hands and restrained their minds, bound them together in misery. Individuals were not allowed to think or do for themselves. Even if they were capable of independent thought to try to better their condition they were confined to their caste or group.

They were restricted and hemmed in by others. The walls had closed in on them and there was no way out.

If a sacred cow trampled their garden and ate their grain, they could do nothing. If a rat were eating precious grain and spreading disease, they could do nothing. Millions and millions of people existed cramped and crowded, regulated and restricted. Many believed they were sacrificing their present lives for a better one in the next reincarnation, so did not complain. Intelligent individual action was all but impossible because individual lives were of no significance. To be poor is by no means pleasant, but to be poor and completely walled-in by religious and government restrictions and by other people who refused to release you seemed unbearable.

Birthright

Without knowing of my emotional and frightened reaction to the study of India one of my teachers took away my fear and made it possible for me to concentrate on the facts of geography. Miss Berg explained that such a way of living couldn't happen to us because there is a difference in the way people think in our country.

"India is a country," she told us, "where a large majority of the people do not see themselves as individuals. Their ancient religions are used to instill a spirit of self-sacrifice. In this country," she went on, "most of us believe that each person is different and each important to himself and God. We are all free to work at any job we can do. We can earn and save, or spend our money. This gives us personal power so we don't have to submit to political power. Instead of being born into a class and dying in the same condition, while good fortune does play some part, we are not dependent on birth or wealth or the government to do well.

"One man in his lifetime can live many lives. He can do many things. He can go from poor to rich, or if he is unlucky, lazy or foolish, from rich to poor. One who begins dependent on the charity of others may some day be able to return the gifts and kindnesses he has received by passing them on to another. We have an inheritance of freedom. We are not limited to one trade or to our father's trade if we do not choose to be. A person who is interested and willing to work can learn many things and have a marvelous personal security if he has many talents. "I teach," she said, "but if I didn't teach I wouldn't starve. I can clerk in a store; I can type letters and take shorthand; I can work in an office; I can see when a job needs to be done and do it without being told. I can organize my work. I have always learned as much as I could because by being well-trained and versatile I am free. That's why I ask you to work so hard. When you grow up I want you to be able to do at least one thing very well, and many things better than most people. Then you will never be enslaved by your ignorance or lack of ability. If you are well prepared for life you will never be fenced in. You will never have to sell your soul to buy your bread."

I wish today's children could learn from a Miss Berg. She might arm them against sociological teaching which robs them of 'self' and soul before they are old enough to know they have been cheated. She might warn them against turning vital economic and social functions over to political and therefore sociological central control. She might warn them against building up government as the one source of wealth, service, supply and power. She might warn them against selling their birthright of freedom and self responsibility to walk into the long narrow room where there is no choice, no freedom to think constructively about one's own welfare, and no escape.

Consciously or by unconscious intuition she understood the dangers and oppression of the sociologist's 'organic society.' She would never have believed it possible that we could be in danger of giving up individuality to become no more than members of the Great Being – Humanity.

The World Runners

I once knew an exceptionally talented young singer. Glen had an outstanding voice, could write songs, had an excellent stage personality, and could put on an effective and entertaining one man TV show. His talent won him jobs, but he couldn't follow through. Most of those who were impressed with his singing and lively personality cooled off on him after a short time. The failing, I believe, which cost him his career in that city was his busy-body mode of operation. He was never content to do his own job and do it well. He was openly critical of the camera men, the director, the announcer, the musicians, the stage manager, and most stupid of all – the sponsor and the way he wanted his product presented. The point is not whether or not Glen was possessed of sufficient genius to be wiser at all these jobs than the professionals, the point is there were many areas of his own performance and of his own personality which could have been sharpened and polished. By paying so much attention to others he was ignoring his own self-improvement. The other people involved in his show were all doing better than adequate job. They didn't need his nagging. While it would not have been out of line for him to ask for a change now and then, or a better angle for a more effective presentation; his criticisms were constant and done with no tact. He had none of the responsibility for the others' work, yet wanted his way to be followed by all of them.

It was so unpleasant to listen constantly to his nagging critical complaining, no one could stand to have him around for very long. He remained in town for about a year and then left in search of recognition and appreciation in other towns. I hope he has become successful somewhere, but unless he changed his method of operation, I doubt it could be in the field of television entertainment.

Sociological teaching is filling the country with young people like Glen, but most of them can't even sing. They believe they are making a wonderful contribution when they sit on the sidelines and parrot sociological gripes. Most often they are not even directly involved in and have no responsibility for the work they criticize. Because they have been taught that 'Humanity' is their responsibility, they are wasting their precious youth pushing and coercing other people, trying to force them to act as a group to solve problems. The only results they can boast are political. They help politicians grasp more power; which means ever greater power for the sociologists who are always behind the scenes whispering in the politicians' ears, and drawing up plans for new laws, restrictions, and intrusions. Always the plans are sociologically engineered to turn the crank which brings the walls closer and closer. The destructive young critics help sociologists apply the squeeze binding individuals to the group for easier control of the universal tribe.

*"It is the business of teachers to run not merely the
school, but the world; and the world will never be truly
civilized until they assume that responsibility."*[14]

The Empty Shell

Teenagers enter sociology classrooms completely unarmed and
vulnerable. They have limited experience, a minimal knowledge of
history, a subordinate position in which they are not free to probe
or contradict, a dependence on the good will of the teacher because
passing grades are necessary for graduation, and no reason to be
suspicious either of what is presented as knowledge or the intent of
the instruction. Few, if any, parents look at their children's books. It
is a beautiful set-up, and sociologists use it to full advantage.

*"The school is the germ plasm of the higher civilization.
Teachers are, therefore, in charge of social selection
at the source of origins for each new generation; they
can even introduce at will mutations of their own
invention."*[15]

No child takes sociology for his own benefit or profit. He may take
it to satisfy his curiosity, because it is required (not needed) for some
field of work which interests him, or because he needs the credits for
graduation; but there is no way personal benefit can be derived from
a sociology class as it might be from an English, mathematics, foreign
language or natural science course. Except for the material sociology
appropriates from other academic areas, there is nothing to be learned
that can be of value to an individual student. The real learning which
might be credited to sociology courses is that which is pirated from
biology, zoology, history, economics, civics, geography, anatomy,
physiology, psychology, etc. A good general science course could
easily convey all the scientific knowledge sociology fences. Stripped
of all its stolen treasures sociology is left with nothing more than a
point of view – the self-denying, de-humanizing, group worshipping,
unscientific, hate-inducing, collective point of view.

Moral Death

Sociologists live in and seek to transport your children to an empty world of make believe. Even their language reveals the artificiality of their approach to life. They talk about 'status' which is one's position in a particular group. They talk about 'role' which is one's manner of performing in the group. It is as if we are all merely actors. These concepts may provide effective phrases in Shakespearean drama, but it is not good to give youngsters the idea that their worth is dependent on artificial 'status' with various groups. It is not good to give children the impression that moral values are merely emotionalized attitudes which are transmitted from parent to child. It is not good to give youngsters the idea that the only reason we refrain from moral wrong is because the group would disapprove if we did not comply with the 'norms.' It is not good to sweep away all that has been discovered or revealed about principles, morality, and personal integrity, and ask children to begin with no greater knowledge than is available to the most backward savage tribes.

How can inexperienced children judge for themselves as sociologists pretend to ask? What child has the knowledge or mature intellect to understand and appreciate the intellectual perfection of the New Testament? How can children feel its emotional satisfaction and appreciate its morally uplifting effect when they have so little experience with life? How can children understand the intellectual exertion, physical suffering, moral turmoil, and resolute conviction which have gone into formulating, understanding, and upholding the principles which enable people to live together in justice and freedom?

Instead of teaching children to seek strength, purpose, truth and independence; sociological training leads to indecision, dependence, artificiality, distortion and moral cowardice. Sociologists have little or no individual moral sense. Morality is forever changing for them because it is whatever 'Society' accepts – whatever appeals to the emotions of the group.

They don't see that what they wish to discard is a great deal more valuable than the 'mores' of a primitive, savage tribe. They reject strong, proven foundations to build on spongy bog. While they talk in hypocritical, pseudo-scientific fashion about social heritage, cultural heritage, and intellectual heritage, they cast away all with no greater consideration than they would give an empty tube of toothpaste. They are willing to forget the moral lessons of past ages. They are willing to forget knowledge, truth, intelligence and reason, for they have been told by their predessors that:

> *"The great secret of the coming age of the world is that civilization rests not on reason but on emotion."*[16]

The Burden

High school students have a great deal to think about, learn and do. They have to think about growing up and planning their futures. They have to think about getting along with their teachers and parents and trying to measure up. They have to think about developing their talents. They have to think about developing their social skills so they can make friends and a proper impression when the opinion of others is important to them. They have to think about their high school sports and high school clubs. They have to learn self-discipline and how to get along with and enjoy the company of the opposite sex. Some have to think about work as they have jobs and special chores. Some have parents who are hard on them – or not hard enough.

The high school years are a time of great activity, personal change and strong emotional pressures, but they should also be a time for fun and a time to build up happy memories.

While some teenagers can find special areas to be helpful to other people, and while most are warm, outgoing and willing to help when asked or when they recognize a need, it is enough. At this very emotional, very difficult, very special and golden time of their lives young people do not need additional mental burdens. They do not need backbiting, gossip, nasty innuendoes, carping criticism. They do not need to be taught to be complainers, critics, gripers, busybodies, trespassers, know-it-alls. They do not need to be shown the unpleasant, negative, failure ridden, spiteful, bitter, depraved, dirty side of life. Most especially they do not need to have the burden for all of the world's failures placed on their shoulders. No one can bear such burdens. If they were older and more experienced they might realize it; but being young many will accept their 'guilt' and 'responsibility' and begin a frantic effort to make things right. Too many instead of choosing an area where they can do constructive work decide that the answer lies in becoming sideline critics and agitators who coerce other people. Instead of building for their own constructive futures, many begin to tear down what others have built. Much of this hysterical destructive attitude is a result of sociological teaching and training.

The Squeeze

It is good that one should give voluntarily from his abundance to elevate others, admirable to share daily bread with those who have none. It is heroic to sacrifice or risk oneself to help another in dire distress. It is constructive to call attention to problems as a challenge to personal excellence giving examples of individuals who have overcome them and made great discoveries, done fine work, developed new and better methods to perform services or produce wanted goods. It is constructive to point out the many areas where young people can do useful, satisfying, productive work, and to inspire a zest for life. It is constructive to give examples of individuals who have sacrificed for a purpose or dedicated their lives to a search for truth, but it is an abomination to teach children they, themselves, have no personal value – that the only way they can prove their worth is to sacrifice themselves to Humanity for the sake of the Universal Tribe – to accept responsibility for all the world's hunger, all the world's poverty, all the world's disease and misery, all the world's ignorance, cares, headaches and battles.

Sociologists place these intolerable and impossible burdens on young people, but give them no avenue of personal achievement which has any hope of accomplishing useful goals. They close doors to productive activity by degrading work for personal gain. They close doors to personal achievement by demanding equality. They clamp the lid on personal happiness by demanding all share everyone's misery. They fill minds with guilt for other people's errors and misdeeds. They offer only collective solutions to personal problems – collective solutions to bind everyone to the group – immobilizing them so individual efforts will be more and more impossible and unproductive.

As the walls are closing in sociologists use the students to help crank them closer and closer. Each new generation has less room to move toward personal goals. They are told their salvation is in the group and in appealing to politicians for group benefits. The students scream and push, march and throw stones in hope of getting political action. All the while sociologists whisper in the politician's ears, "Take more power. Take more control. We will tell you what to do. We are the scientists. We will rule through you." The politicians listen, obey, and the walls move closer.

The Greater Tribe

Those things which free minds and promote individual development and self-control are most frequently degraded by sociologists. Those things which blind the senses, close one's mind, increase dependence, and promote submission are elevated by sociological teaching.

Sociologists have a word which may have done more to break down family loyalty, patriotism, Christian morality, school spirit, fraternal devotion, national and racial pride, artistic appreciation, and scientific honesty than any other term ever invented. The word: Ethnocentric. To sociologists (since they don't like to acknowledge individuals) it means judging other groups in terms of our group's standards. To the students they teach it means, 'Don't accept the values your Christian or Jewish parents may have taught you. If one is proud of and speaks well of his country, family, friends, race, nationality, religion, associations; if he has values and ethical yardsticks for judging others, he is 'ethnocentric.' Ethnocentric groups according to sociologists do not understand other groups and cultures because they judge in terms of their own values and not in terms of the other group's values.

We would understand other cultures better if we judged them from their point of view rather than our own. For example: The Eskimo who kills for revenge is not a criminal, but is admired by his group. The kindly New Guinean head hunter should be understood. Our values do not apply to his culture. He should not be condemned. He believes he needs other men's heads so his children can have names and identities. Premarital pregnancy is not necessarily bad. It is expected of the Bantoc women in the Philippines. It proves them fertile and makes them better marriage prospects. In some cultures it is a friendly gesture for a man to offer the use of his wife to a visiting stranger. We must not look down on these people merely because they have a different set of customs. Many of the practices which seem repugnant to us are necessary to the integration of their society. Morality is only a matter of what is expedient in a given situation or society.

If you have wondered why many young people have abandoned moral principles consider the possibility it might be because sociologists and sociologically oriented teachers tell them morality is just a matter of cultural orientation. They are also told 'society' is changing its orientation and now no longer condemns many practices which were once considered immoral.

> *"Traditionally there was little question that the schools should promote such values as the following:*

1. Respect Property.
2. Be respectful of adults.
3. Say please and thank you at appropriate times.
4. Do not use profane language or bad grammar.
5. Be neat and clean.
6. Do not lie or cheat.

> *Now, however, in some situations these are quite controversial. Many lawsuits and community controversies have focused on the meaning of 'neat and clean,' for example. Several recent surveys indicate that cheating in school, rather than being unacceptable, has become the norm, and most students feel no guilt about cheating. Standards of profanity are constantly changing and words that one rarely heard used in public a few years ago are now heard a great deal. While many may not like these developments, it is very necessary for teachers to recognize that they are taking place.[17]*

Don't expect sociologists to explain to your children that the primitive 'cultures' which they seek to emulate value only the 'tribe' and the 'group,' that individual lives are not considered. Don't expect the sociologists to worry about the Eskimo who lost his life, the tribesman who lost his head, the baby who never knew his father and a father's personal protection, and the wife who must accept violation from every male who comes to visit. And don't expect the sociologists to worry about what their teaching does to your children! The sociologists are trying to build a world tribal society. They must attend to their work!

Alienation of Affection

It is becoming ever more painful to read the daily paper. Nearly every day in most cities – large or small – there are stories of youths and girls who have lost their search for 'identity.' Some have died from drug overdoses; some in drug-crazed stupor have taken their own lives; some have turned to crime and prostitution; others look for 'status' and identity in mob action and destructive agitation. There are parents who don't need newspapers to come close to the pain because their own children or those of close friends and relatives are lost and confused.

The deluded children say they hate life, hate 'society,' hate all the pretense and hypocrisy, hate their teachers, their parents, their country. These poor unhappy ones do not know it, but it is not life they hate, not pride of achievement, not their families, nor their country, but the barren futility of the sociologist's way of looking at life, - the negative, unkind, uncharitable, distorted sociological view of life.

Family life because it develops individual personality and because a family is a strong economic unit is a prime target of sociologists. It is not difficult to drive a wedge between a child and his parents by pointing out parental defects to the child. We all have faults. Some parents are selfish; some lack self-control; others are tactless, domineering and have unattractive vices; some parents are not as loving or interested as they might be; but children are robust and resilient. They forget and forgive and learn. Most of them would be O.K. if they had only their parents' human imperfections to contend with. Even bad television and x-rated books, magazines, and movies need not destroy them if their schools inspired them, reinforced their virtues, taught them their individual worth and respected the parent-child relationship. If the warm, loving side of the parental picture were pointed out it might help children be happy, honest, conscientious, appreciative and productive.

Even if some homes are not the best, or especially because some homes are not the best, the school should never cut down a child's parents, never say destructive things about them in the child's presence. The only one harmed by such malicious talk is the child. No child should be put in the position of having to defend his parents' imperfections to that teacher. He should never be put on the defensive in this manner. There is no way a child can benefit.

When a person is older and a parent himself, he may seek information on how to raise his own children, but none of the destructive type talk which goes on in a sociology classroom, or in a sociologically oriented primary school is appropriate for little children or high school students – nor is it appropriate at the college level where parents should be able to expect a little more than a stab in the back. Even a psychology teacher can discuss good and bad influences without making blanket accusations against parents.

There may be a great deal of truth in the statement that delinquent children frequently come from undesirable homes, but there is no excuse for making such a statement to children who are in the process of developing their own characters and personalities. Such broad statements and even discussion of juvenile delinquency to juveniles in the manner sociologists adopt can only serve to call attention to the fact that such types of behavior are open to them. This talk also serves to justify wrong behavior. Youngsters feel they can escape responsibility for their own acts by blaming family influences.

Children are extremely impressionable. If one were to make a statement to a large class that some children take poison because they are curious or that some children take poison because they are angry with their parents; sure as day follows night some kids would try poison.

If there is one thing I know after teaching and living with teen-aged boys and girls, it is that they are not yet objective about themselves.

All teenagers have some problems and most of them during unhappy times believe they are being treated unfairly. While they have a marvelous sense of humor, few are ready to laugh at themselves or adopt a philosophical attitude about their own faults and errors. They tend to take everything personally, and most certainly are *not* ready for objective classroom discussions about teen-aged behavior and parent-child relationships.

Imagine a young person who is going through a difficult time emotionally. How do you think he might react upon finding statements similar to the following in his sociology textbook?

Most Children's Problems Have Their Roots in the Family.

Sociologists Talk About Problem Parents Rather Than Problem Children.

The Child Attacks Other Children When His Needs Are Not Met By Parents.

It Is Not Surprising That Many Children Spend Little Time At Home Or Run Away From Home.

All Young People Must Break Away From The Family.

Conflict in the Family Is Not Always The Parents' Fault.

Parents of the 'Ordering and Forbidding' School Are Likely To Have Real Conflict.

Truancy Indicates The Home Lacks Authority.

A Parents' Lack of Understanding May Be Responsible For A Child's Juvenile Delinquency.

Just Because You Were Reared In An Unhappy Home Is No Reason Your Children Should Be.

Low Family Social Standing And Income Block Some Children's Opportunities.

Parents Pass On Their Own Feelings Of Prejudice To Their Children.

The Child Has No Chance To Judge For Himself.

No One Is Fully Victimized By His Family.

The Rejected Boy May Turn To Stealing, Speeding Or Dare-Devil Activities.

A Girl Who Has Been Denied Affection At Home Sometimes Seeks Satisfaction Through Sex Delinquency.

The Child Has No Chance To Judge For Himself.

Do you want your children upset by such vindictive criticism and influenced by such destructive suggestions? Why would sociologists want to call attention to and blame so many troubles on parents; and then suggest running away or delinquent behavior as a solution. What is the purpose of risking creating new difficulties by such intemperate discussions with impressionable youngsters?

If you want to discover the answers to these questions you can't be too polite or too charitable. Read your sociology book very carefully. You will learn who wants to be there to solve all the problems created: the sociologically trained and oriented workers. In behalf of 'Society' they are ready to pick up the pieces and take control. Child destruction and alienating children from parents and parents' opinions are just other ways of weakening family bonds and gaining sociological power. Whether your children are destroyed physically, morally, or intellectually is of little consequence to the child corrupters. It is only important that new generations be cleansed of the 'insanity of individualism' which might interfere with their socialization.

If a youngster leaves his sociology course with no other impression, the course will have been successful from a sociological point of view if he believes parents are inadequate, sociologists are needed to understand and solve the problems of the world, and that all personal problems have collective solutions.

> *"If customs or institutions are to be reformed it is first necessary to dig for them new channels of popular belief. Secure the prevalence of new beliefs and new programs of collective behavior will result; indeed, not otherwise can social changes be originated – except by sheer coercion."*[18]

Indirect Alienation

There are direct ways and indirect ways to damage a child's respect for his parents. Sociologists, as you have seen, do not scorn the direct methods, but indirect methods are also useful to them. When they enter into discussions of status they can damage a child's regard for his parents and also narrow his own field of choice when considering future careers. Some books go to the outrageous extreme of listing anywhere from fifty to one hundred occupations. The occupations are rated on the basis of prestige and status. If Dad is a Supreme Court Justice, a physician, state governor, cabinet member, diplomat, scientist, banker or professor, he has extremely high social prestige and status. If he is a bookkeeper, insurance agent or undertaker, that's about average. If he is a barber, milkman, or truck driver, his status in society is below average. If he is a dock worker, night watchman, janitor, garbage collector or shoe shiner his status couldn't be much lower.

Imagine the effect on children of such nonsensical unscientific games! A very small percentage of the children will have fathers in the 'upper status' groups. They are encouraged to feel superior, perhaps a little guilty, and possibly isolated to some degree from their classmates. Those whose fathers are said to have average prestige may not be damaged too much by the revelation other than to begin to develop a resentment against a 'society' that values people on such shallow grounds. Now consider the children who are told their fathers have the lowest status. Can they whose fathers' occupations have been insulted in front of their classmates fail to feel humiliation and resentment? The resentment is not likely to be directed against the teacher, book, or sociologist who dreamed up the malignant little exercise, but against their fathers or against 'society' for so insulting the dearly-beloved, hard-working dads.

There are also children who may hear in sociology class that their fathers are similar to helpless senseless robots because they work in factories. If a child sits in class and allows his father's occupation to be discussed in such a manner he is damaged. If he makes a protest he has to risk admitting before his classmates that his father is like a helpless senseless robot. What a nasty, cruel, unnecessary choice to force on a child. Where is the respect that every hard-working responsible worker deserves?

A moment's thought would make the ridiculousness of the sociological idea that machines enslave people and turn them into robots immediately apparent. If men use shovels to dig a ditch, are they slaves to the shovels because they are not clawing the dirt with their hands?

The resentment built up by discussion of status and by the degrading of occupations can be used by sociologists. In later life those who have been wounded or have guilty feelings may be more responsive to sociological prodding for laws to restrict opportunities. They may be more willing to help crank the sociologists' restrictive walls even closer.

Consciousness of Kind

One sociological lie has been used with stunning effectiveness to discredit parents in the eyes of their children and also to build up hate between people of different races so they can be played one against another. Guilt for this vicious distortion can be laid directly at the door of sociologists who represent it to students as truth. They know better, yet they lie. The lie is so widespread and socially acceptable I risk losing some readers by discussing it; but because parents are treated with contempt because of it by the sociological trainers of their children, I think the risk is worth taking.

Perhaps I am more aware of the sociological distortion because it is related to one of my earliest and at the time most frightening childhood memories. I was just three. I was walking up the back stairway of the building where my parents had rented an apartment when I heard footsteps. Suddenly a person appeared on the landing above me – big and black with large white eyes and flashing white teeth. I was petrified with fright. As she came closer she began to speak and I panicked. Terror stricken and screaming hysterically, I shot back down the stairs straight to my mother's arms. I knew she wouldn't let that big woman eat me.

Of course the poor lady was hurt by my action and sorry she had frightened me. She loved children and had only smiled and started to say 'Good morning' when I commenced my screaming session. But I had never seen a negro person before. Not only did she appear suddenly, but there was an obvious difference between her and all the other people I had seen up to that time. Nobody had told me to *notice* this difference. Nobody *told* me to be frightened of her. Meeting her was a new experience and I was afraid.

My mother spent much time explaining to me that this was a kind woman who loved little girls – that she would never hurt me and was only being friendly. She told me I would see many more black people during our stay in Philadelphia, and I was not to be frightened.

I didn't come around right away. There was another incident in a cafeteria because I was alone when the colored bus boy came to clear the table. But by the time we left Philadelphia six weeks later I was a much better-behaved little girl.

From my own experience I know that it is not true that racial differences would be unnoticed if parents didn't teach their children to fear, hate or avoid other races. Quite the opposite is true. We are wary of one another until we are reassured. It is natural to feel safer and more comfortable with those who are like ourselves. The ancient Greek poets said, "Birds of a feather flock together." Sociologists, despite their lies, recognize this truth and among themselves call it 'consciousness of kind.'

> "*The original and elementary subjective fact in society is the consciousness of kind. By this term I mean a state of consciousness in which any being, whether low or*

high in the scale of life, recognizes another conscious being as of like kind with itself."[19]

Sociological Solidarity

More than any others, it is the sociologists and sociologically oriented who are offended by the fact that people come in different colors. It is they who tell us we should be 'color blind.' Color blind – indeed! Hypocritical is the word! How can we be friends when we begin our friendship with a lie and a refusal to recognize one another's attributes? Are racial differences so offensive we have to close our eyes and not look at each other? Are we to be so blind to our own identity we cannot recognize or must be offended by our own color?

Sociologists can't tolerate differences. Racial differences particularly, are offensive because they interfere with sociological 'solidarity.' It would be easier for sociologists to take control if the black people would just disappear. Then we would be more alike and more willing to be integrated and treated as indistinguishable members of the greater body.

> "*The blinding vision of which the west has caught sight has been that there is but one class, and but one color, and but one soul in humanity.*"[20]

To a sociologically oriented individual the preceeding thought is beautiful and inspiring. Hundreds of millions of bodies and one soul for all! All they need do if this concept be accepted is put themselves in control of the master soul.

The sociological advance is occurring more easily in countries such as China and Sweden in which the differences between people are less pronounced than they are in our country. Thank the Lord for variety! The fact that our country is composed of people of such diversity may have helped retard the sociological domination.

While there are wide differences we are not isolated. Emotional, intellectual and spiritual likenesses draw us to other people. A mother who loves her children and wants to protect them sympathizes with and wants to help other mothers and their children. Admiration for talent, intelligence, character, courage and congeniality draws people together. The desire to trade goods and services draws people together. The mental and spiritual likenesses are often a great deal more significant than the physical differences.

But the differences are there. They exist. Noticing them – even talking about them is not a sign of hate. However, consider those who reject the very idea of variety and individual souls – do they not hate us all? Do they not strive to turn us all in mindless, soulless, assembly-line robot slaves?

> *"The purpose of this chapter is to emphasize the responsibility of education for making us all alike."*[21]

Sociological De-Humanization

Sociological de-humanization begins with the child in the womb. In the sociological point of view the new life which is developing is not human – nor is the child human when it is born. It must *become* human through socialization. This is the function of the Group or Society.

Perhaps the sociology text you have acquired is one which will continue the explanation of this concept with examples of 'wild' children who were more like animals because they had been deprived of group interaction. Sociologists would have one believe that because these poor young 'creatures' had been unable to acquire the talents and self-control which we learn from our parents and from others, they are on a level with beasts.

What if a child's arms and legs were bound at birth so he could never exercise his muscles? What if he managed to survive, but because his muscles were never exercised they atrophied and became useless? Would that mean his body was not a human body? Of course not. The human attributes were there. This does not mean they cannot be destroyed or deprived of the opportunity to develop.

The fact that an infant needs adult help to survive does not deprive that infant of his human identity. The fact that he learns from his parents and others does not deprive him of his independent mind. The fact that he is taught self-control does not deprive him of his individual freedom. The fact that he learns from past and present generations does not place him in eternal bondage and cement him to all of 'Humanity.' Individuals of each generation reap what previous generations have sown – to their profit if they harvest wisely as in the case of many discoveries which have made our lives more comfortable and productive, or to their degradation if they accept untruth and corruption which ignorant or cunning predecessors bequeath. There is no profit for us or our children in the cannibalistic sociological religion. Would we could decline that part of our heritage!

The Prize

Plain stupidity may be forgivable, but teaching stupidity with full knowledge of the fact that it is stupidity and teaching it for the purpose of corrupting and enslaving the innocent and unsuspecting students is a deed monstrous beyond description.

While I suspect most of the teachers of sociology are as much victims of the sociological religion as their students, the top intellectuals in the field know what they are doing and why. They know they are training future adults with a slave mentality – adults who will be little more than obedient zombies, who have no self-esteem, who can easily be used as pawns to help bring about complete sociological submission. Here are some of the ways sociologists teach children they are unimportant and ineffective as individuals:

1. By telling them moral maturity means to become less ego-centered and more Society-centered.
2. By telling them they are not human until Society makes them so.
3. By telling them they have no 'self' until Society gives it to them.
4. By telling them there is little chance that young people of average intelligence will ever make an impressive contribution to Man's store of knowledge and skill.
5. By leaving out or downgrading the important motivations for personal achievement: the satisfaction of a scientific curiosity, the desire to learn about the wonders of nature, the desire to acquire something of value and to have a surplus to exchange with other individuals, the desire to bring gifts to family and loved ones, the desire to be useful to other people, and the feeling of personal satisfaction for a job well done. No, the

main sociological motivation for personal achievement is to gain 'status' in Society.

My God! Can they then pretend to wonder why young people have lost ambition and the spark of life which drives them to higher achievement?

Status in Society! – Such a prize! The young victims surely sense there must be something more to life than 'status in Society.' But who is to tell them if their teachers do not, and if in addition they interpret the motives of parents in the same shallow terms and down grade their accomplishments?

Where can a child go for inspiration? – for a sense of wonder? – for training in personal moral conduct? – for an appreciation of his heritage? – for lessons in courage? – Where is teaching the truth and real values? Where can a child go for uncorrupted knowledge?

Training

Nearly a year ago my husband and I made an emotional decision which we regretted many times since. The children came home from their cousin's with the most appealing, beautifully-marked, perky-looking German shepherd puppy any of us had ever seen. We all knew what raising a puppy meant for the appearance of our beautiful garden, how the house would probably suffer from the puppy's bad habits, the trials that would be ahead, the cold and rainy mornings when someone would have to attend to the dog's needs, but we pushed all this from our minds. The puppy got to us, and that was it.

He chewed the woodwork, tore the wallpaper off the wall, destroyed a portable radio, turned a sweater into shredded yarn, but the habit that infuriated me and made me feel helpless, stupid and frustrated was his refusal to come when I called. He never went far as long as I was present, but he would duck and dodge and run around the bushes, then cut out across the neighbor's yard. He'd drink out of her birdbath until I got within two feet of him, and then take off the instant I reached out. Whenever I was in no mood for games he kept it up longer. He drove me wild. But that wasn't the only reason we decided we needed a trainer. When Baron was about eight months old the gas man came to read the meter. I learned then that our *weak moment* was going to be more than just a family pet. His protective instincts took over completely. He lunged at the poor man with all the ferocity of a killer wolf. Luckily the man had not quite entered the house and was able to close the screen door before Baron sampled his flesh, but the encounter convinced us that if we couldn't master the dog, he would have to go.

Our trainer, who was familiar with our dog's family tree, informed us Baron's reaction to intrusion was good and to be expected since he came from three generations of trained guard dogs. Knowing that fact did nothing to dispel my apprehension about the dog's future disposition, but we were assured he could be trained to give immediate obedience and to stay on our property.

We all participated, and Baron learned to heel, to sit and lie down on command, to jump over barriers and return immediately to his trainer. He learned that every human in the family outranked him and that he would have to conform to our rules. The training made him a great deal easier to live with.

In the early training he began to be somewhat better outside. He would respond quickly to a man's voice, but I still had difficulty. That is, I had difficulty until I learned to use the throwing chain. The throwing chain is a moderately heavy circular chain of about twelve or fourteen links. When Baron decides to run off, the chain is thrown at him. He has no idea where it comes from, and doesn't understand the hit, but he is immediately subdued. He stops dead. The next command is obeyed instantly. Two or three hits were all it took, and now it is seldom necessary to throw the chain. All that is needed is to rattle it and he obeys. If Baron shows the least doubt about being willing to obey, the chain is thrown at his back just as he starts to take off. There is instant obedience and the power of a mere rattle of the chain is reinforced.

Such training is wonderful for dogs. Baron knows his place and keeps to it. He is not a danger to visitors to our house, and he is obedient both inside and out. We can live with our 'mistake' and even begin to admit it might not have been so terrible an error after all. He is a superb watchdog and a good friend to everyone in the family. He is happy and we are much relieved.

Children need training too. They need training in personal habits, self-control, cleanliness and proper care of their surroundings, and they need training to teach them the type of behavior which has been proven over many generations to be good moral behavior. But their training should be of the type that can be rationally explained when they are able to understand. Children are not animals and should not be trained for a lifetime of instant irrational obedience. Unthinking submission and follow-the-group morality are not worthy goals for humans. Self-respecting parents will train their children for future freedom and independence. As each year passes the children are permitted to be more and more responsible for themselves.

Few, if any, parents are perfect, but children have a better chance for free and happy lives under natural parental control than any artificial arrangement sociologists can concoct, because parents let go. Parents recognize their children's lives are their own. Sociologists train for lifetime submission and obedience. Individuals exist only for the good of the greater whole – collective Humanity. To sociologists individuals are 'human resources' to be exploited for collective purposes.

Socioligical Throwing Chains

If intelligent people are to become tools of slavemasters, the power and protection of children's natural trainers – their parents and legitimate agents of their parents – has to be broken. Then means have to be found to make new generations submissive to trainers who teach them blind obedience.

The slave trainers have been working in our country for well over 100 years. It has taken a long time and a great deal of work and planning for them to reach the present stage of control over education. Each new generation has produced more individuals of a slave mentality. Many converts have been made at the top intellectual levels because those who fancied themselves brilliant and above the 'masses' saw themselves as leaders; and at the lower intellectual levels because it is difficult to understand bondage without visible chains and seduction by the bearers of gifts.

Intelligent, hard-working, self-respecting, productive individuals who envision themselves as neither master nor slave are becoming more and more aware of the squeeze as their choices are limited. Yet they have appeared to accept encroachments on personal liberty. This has not been due to a lack of courage or unwillingness to sacrifice for principle, but to an honest bewilderment about the moral principles involved and how to meet the issue. True principles have been obscured by political oratory and counterfeit 'values' have been substituted. The values of sociological thinkers have been used by them in the same manner I use the throwing chain on Baron. Every time they want to restrict individual range of action, or if there is an opportunity for some to break free the sociological trainers hurl one of their chains. Sometimes they only need rattle it and we heel.

Unless we are able to render the sociological trainer's values or throwing chains powerless to affect our behavior, and unless we can prevent them from training our children to respond to these false religious values, our lives and our children's lives will increasingly become lives of turmoil and suppression.

The trick, then, is to stop cringing when one of the chains is thrown, to become impassive when it hits, deaf when we hear it rattle. One who is aware of what to expect is not nearly so likely to be intimidated.

Equality

The most effective, most frequently used, hardest to combat sociological throwing chain is the dogma of equality. Equality is taught to children as a supreme value. It is an hallucination, an ideal that can never be realized – only emotionalized and held before the eyes to blind the vision.

> *"The science of the emotion of the ideal is the science of power in civilization...."*[22]

> *"Once the influence of the ideal is imposed upon the individual by social heredity,...he can never escape from it. It is this creation of the ideal, and the organization of the minds upon which it is imposed into the collective will, that constitute the first objective in the science of power in the future of the world."*[23]

The dogma of equality is the most powerful throwing chain of those used to train children to act according to sociological bidding. Unless they are freed from this dogma, your children, their children, and their children's children could be sociologically enslaved. The word has achieved a near-religious acceptance to the point where its truth is taken on faith and seldom questioned. Yet, nowhere in nature does it exist.

The closest thing I have ever seen to human 'equality' is in the case of identical twins. Yet, among all the identical twins I have known, I could by careful observation easily distinguish one from the other. Each wanted to be treated as an individual, not as half of a pair.

Dictators can keep most subjects on a more equal economic level than can be accomplished if government powers are limited, but still there are at least two classes: those who are supposed to be equal, and the equalizers.

People who wish to use and act on their individual intelligence and to seek their own destiny cannot keep their integrity if they make equality their goal. In the name of equality they would be sacrificing the right of each to govern his own life.

Freedom and enforced equality are irreconcilable opposites. Efforts to force economic and social equality only restrict freedom, thought, intelligence and productive capacity. Equality as a goal or dogma is a crippler and a killer.

Equality Is -----

Equality is the ceiling above which one dare not rise; the mental block which holds one back from superior accomplishment.

Equality is hate for your superiors and contempt for your inferiors.

Equality is the yoke which binds us to the failures, degenerates and primitives of the world, and the wedge which separates us from the inspiration of the hard-working, successful, and morally pure.

Equality, the sociologists' supreme value, is the source of guilt for material abundance; the excuse for oppression; the promise, which because it cannot be kept, enslaves its believers.

Equality is the denial of nature, the rallying cry of the willfully blind, the source of poetic inspiration for men without dreams; the ever-gushing source of tear-stained rhetoric for hypocritical politicians who seek power.

Equality is morality for the morally bankrupt.

Equality is the carrot and the stick – the sociologists' goal for all who are not sociologists; and the sociologists' justification for the whip to punish those who dare achieve beyond sociologically prescribed limits.

Equality is the narrow room where sociologists cast all the world's people, then crank the walls closer.

Equality is death of spirit, choice denied.

Equality is never saying, "Look where I came from. See where I am!"

Equality is waking up every day of your life with no place to go.

Equality is thinking always about other people – about whether they have more than you, or you have more than they.

Equality is judging everyone the same, loving everyone the same HATING everyone the same.

Equality is no mountains to climb, no barriers to leap, no dreams to make real.

Equality is spying on other people to be sure they have not become unequal.

Equality is dragging down the ones who climb too high.

Equality is taking away from those who have too much.

Equality is seeing yourself no better than the most corrupt and no less than the most virtuous.

Equality is wanting no more and no less than anyone on earth, achieving no more no less than anyone; giving no more no less than anyone; hoping no more no less than anyone.

Equality is having no more joy than anyone and as much sorrow as everyone.

Equality as an ideal shuts out reason, closes doors, denies nature and reality.

Equality as a demand can turn potentially kind considerate charitable people into aggressive snarling beasts.

Equality as a value replaces individual virtues of love, kindness, honesty, industry, truth, freedom, morality, faith, hope and charity.

Equality is a zombie, head lowered, never daring to look up, ahead, or to the side – marching at measured pace with all who deny individuality and self.

Equality, if the sociologists have their way, is what we will bequeath to our children.

The Magic Word

Politically the word 'equality' has worked like a voodoo charm. All a politician needs to do is shout 'equality' and the opposition crumbles away to whatever new plan for the consolidation of sociological power is being pushed.

Why must we accept sociological control over medical care?

EQUALITY

Why must we suffer sociological economic manipulation?

EQUALITY

Why have sociologists been granted control over education?

EQUALITY

Why should our possessions and hard-earned income be given away to primitives and strangers all over the world without our consent?

EQUALITY

Why should tiny tots be taken away from their mothers for sociological training before they are five?

EQUALITY

Why should youngsters be forcibly transported to school many miles from home against their parents' wishes and away from their supervision?

EQUALITY

Why should academic standards be lowered?

EQUALITY

Why should entrants to the professions no longer be chosen on the basis of intellectual achievement, good character and willingness to invest in their own future?

EQUALITY

Why should productive people be compelled to do more for the unproductive than they are willing to do for themselves?

EQUALITY

Who supervises all this equality and determines what laws should be passed to punish inequality?

By now, I believe you know.

The New Conscience

Sociologists have discovered that there are two types of conscience. The old-style conscience which they believe is obsolete and unfitted to present day life is the authoritarian conscience. The new up-to-date 'practical' conscience which they are now trying to convince teachers to develop in your children is the rational conscience.

> "A child generally comes to school with what J.J. Havighurst calls an authoritarian conscience acquired from his parents through a progression of punishments and rewards. He soon learns that he is not equipped to deal with all the new situations which confront him. Peers and teachers join and sometimes supplant parents in helping him to find solutions which are often in conflict with those offered by his parents. His task, then is to change from this early authoritarian conscience to a rational one."[24]

The old-style authoritarian conscience was positive, knew what was right and what was wrong. The rational conscience expresses doubt and looks for reasons to justify whatever behavior is chosen. One must think about his behavior and explain to himself why he acted as he did, or why he intends to act in a certain way.

Since the rational conscience responds to reason, it is a great deal easier to deal with. To change a decision of one who has a rational conscience all you have to do is provide justification strong enough to break his resistance. It doesn't require very strong arguments to collapse the conscience of a young person if it is built only on his own meager experience, education and reasoning power. Once cut off from historical and religious morality a youngster with a rational conscience is hopelessly adrift. There are always good reasons for doing wrong.

If it is true that young girls are more easily seduced today, the new rational conscience provided through the courtesy of their sociological education could be largely to blame. There are always lots of good reasons to submit, but a young woman with an authoritarian conscience never listened or took them seriously. She didn't have to provide reasonable excuses for saying no. She just said no. While she may have enjoyed and been amused by the intellectual sparring, she never took it seriously.

An authoritarian conscience may be, as the sociologists suggest, the result of parental and religious influences, but it is not as they claim the result of blind obedience. It is the result of centuries of experience, knowledge and intuition passed on with love from parent to child. It is based on a confident belief that one's moral behavior and his own self-respect are among the most important of life's values – more important than material goods or the opinion of others.

While a person with an authoritarian conscience does not always listen to that conscience, and may make many mistakes in his lifetime; he knows they are mistakes. He knows when he has done wrong. The conscience is not deceived. He will ask that his errors and faults be forgiven, but he would never expect or want them to be justified.

The rational conscience thinks about the possibilities and chooses the most useful course at any particular moment based only on his own reason and emotions. The most important thing to a rational conscience is not what decision is made, but that the decision was arrived at by conscious thought. It is a flexible conscience which can be made to justify any type behavior which appears reasonable. It responds to public opinion and the needs of Society. And herein lies its usefulness to sociologists who see themselves as Society's guardians.

Facts of Life

In recent years there has been much argument and turmoil over the issue of bringing special courses in sex education into the schools. In the heat of argument one aspect is escaping most people. Formerly some sex education was included in science courses, physical education courses, home economics courses, and even in English courses through reading of literature such as *THE SCARLET LETTER,* etc. Bits of information could be gradually assimilated by students without the necessity of getting deeply involved in discussions of personal matters in an impersonal situation.

If, as claimed, more information about reproduction was necessary it could easily have been included in already existing science courses under human anatomy and physiology. Teaching could perhaps have gone quite a bit farther without becoming offensive. This, however, would not have served the sociological purpose.

For years "Marriage and the Family" courses have been a part of the college curriculum offered by the sociology departments at universities. It is therefore logical to assume that in the majority of grade and high schools which adopt sex education courses the teaching will be in the hands of 'social science' teachers or sociologically trained and oriented teachers rather than teachers of natural science. As years pass it will become the exclusive prerogative of sociologists to do the training in sexual facts and morality. They have wanted this power for a long time, and are now beginning to realize it.

> "But most of all, must social religion demand a complete change in our 'mores' with reference to marriage and the family. Instead of regarding these as matters of individual convenience, social religion must teach that they are social responsibilities and also opportunities for human service. The whole family life must be put upon an ethical instead of a selfish basis. Marriage itself should come to symbolize, both in the minds of the contracting parties and of the community, full consecration of life to the service of the race."[25]

Chapter III

Tomorrow

"Eugenics demands that we control marriage in the interests of the race, but this in turn implies the control of all sex relations."[26]

Conclusion of the Hate Factory

It is enough. IT IS TIME TO CALL A HALT. Too many children have already been corrupted. If we do not begin now to rescue our children from the persuaders in the hate factories and reclaim our parental rights they may be lost to parents for centuries to come.

Remember, whatever your race or religion; no matter what sins you have committed in the past; regardless of whether you are sometimes too harsh, too lenient, too distracted, too lazy, too uneducated, too overeducated, too prejudiced, too nervous, too unhappy, too poor, too rich, too sick, or even too drunk to be an ideal parent – if you love your children and are aware that there is a difference between right and wrong, and are trying to teach that difference to your children; you are most certainly a better guardian and are better equipped to guide your children than any cynical, sociologically-dominated educator whose good judgment is blinded by his messianic illusions.

It is time to be a jealous parent – to do everything in your power to keep your children's education and moral training in your own hands;

to refuse to allow teachers to teach or speak to your children in such a manner as to alienate their affection; to forbid the moral corruption of your children by the sociological religion and sociology's rational conscience; to insure that your children gain a respect for truth and intellectual integrity.

Rescuing young people from sociology and sociologically-oriented classes is more important than a high school or college diploma, more important than 'status' in society, more important than 'group solidarity.' To reject sociology is the first step toward maintaining and regaining individual worth, integrity, and freedom, self-respect and knowledge of one's own human identity.

Sociology and sociologists have a strong grip on education in schools at all levels in every part of the country. But as a parent you are not powerless. There are many courses of action open to you even before the principles of religious liberty on which the country was founded are effectively restored.

If you can afford it and a good alternative is available withdraw your children from sociologically oriented anti-parental schools and place them in schools which recognize individual worth and liberty.

If you cannot withdraw your children from such schools, insist that they be excused from sociology classes and sociologically-oriented studies. Also write a letter to their school and keep a copy for yourself in which you state that your children are not to be indoctrinated in any class with the 'values' of the sociological religion, and that you forbid them to be used for sociological testing, experimentation or indoctrination.

If you are not ready to withdraw your children from sociology classes, suggest this book be used as a supplementary text.

If you cannot convince the school officials to use this book as a means to present a balanced view of sociology, consult your children's individual teachers. They may be open to the suggestion and willing to point out the intent and methods of sociology by teaching from a more informed point of view.

If there seems to be no way for you to do any of the above, and if you feel you cannot change the school situation in which your children are confined, warn the children themselves about the influences they are likely to encounter so they will not be completely vulnerable because of ignorance.

Whatever course you choose, have the courage to stand alone if you must, remembering others are doing the same. But don't wait for the 'group' to act. As our individual numbers increase, one day soon our paths may meet, and cross, and branch out until the work of the Hate Factories is understood and overcome by loving parents everywhere.

Chapter IV

Up Date

The Hate Factory is not the last word. It is only a primer. Every day since its initial publication in 1972 new information has come to my attention. It is impossible to include all I would like you to know to bring you up-to-date. However, one of the trends you should be aware of to protect yourself and those you love is the rapid re-naming of sociologists and sociologically-oriented instructors. Because sociology is being exposed as nothing more than a technique to gain power over people, sociologists have had to adopt new methods and new terminology. Many sociologists, humanists, and sociologically-indoctrinated teachers and curriculum planners now call themselves 'futurists.' Sociology classes are more and more being called 'future education', 'futuristics', or studies in 'alternative futures'. These classes are heavily financed by the federal government.

Pretending to study the future is a devilishly clever way to present sociological ideas in an exciting new format. Students are fascinated by science-fiction and by all the attention paid to their own predictions about the future. Futurism is a devious way to destroy character, principles and moral standards. Immorality is presented as the morality of the future. International collectivism is palmed off as the social order of the future. Students are also told technology is changing the world so fast that the governments must take steps to slow it down. The students become frightened and willing to give the governments more power over their lives so they will be safe from the frightening new sociologically-invented disease called 'future shock.'

Students of all ages are being changed and corrupted in courses on the future. I cannot overemphasize the necessity for avoiding such courses and for keeping your children out of them. Even innocent-appearing science-fiction is now being used on a massive scale to indoctrinate and corrupt the reader.

I am including here a list of 'Don'ts' for students which appeared recently in my "Truth In Education" column in THE MILWAUKEE COUNTY NEWS. I hope you will be guided by the warnings and be more alert to the harmful influences in education because of them.

DON'TS FOR STUDENTS

DON'T get into science-fiction values discussions or trust a teacher who dwells on science-fiction in his 'teaching'.

DON'T discuss the future or future social arrangements or governments in class.

DON'T discuss values.

DON'T write a family history.

DON'T answer personal questions or questions about members of your family.

DON'T play blindfolded games in class.

DON'T exchange 'opinions' on political or social issues.

DON'T write an autobiography.

DON'T keep a journal of your opinions, activities and feelings.

DON'T take intelligence tests. Write tests only on your lessons. Force others to judge you on personal achievement.

DON'T discuss boy-girl or parent-child relationships in class.

DON'T confide in teachers, particularly sociology or social studies and English teachers.

DON'T judge a teacher by his appearance or personality, but on his competence as a teacher of solid knowledge.

DON'T think a teacher is doing you a favor if he gives you a good grade for poor work or in useless subjects.

DON'T join any social action or social work groups.

DON'T take 'social studies' or 'future studies'. Demand course definition: history, geography, civics, French, English, etc.

DON'T role play or participate in socio-dramas.

DON'T worry about the race or color of your classmates. Education is of the mind, not the body.

DON'T get involved in school-sponsored or government-sponsored exchange or camping programs which place you in the homes of strangers.

DON'T be afraid to say 'no' to morally corrupting literature games and activities in class.

DON'T submit to psychological testing.

DON'T fall for books like *Future Shock* which are intended to put readers in a state of panic about 'change' so they will be willing to accept slavery. Advances in science and technology don't drive people into shock. It is government and vain-brain intrusions in private lives which cause much of the unbalance in nature and in people.

DON'T get into classroom discussions which begin:
WHAT WOULD YOU DO IF....?
WHAT IF....?
SHOULD WE....?
DO YO USUPPOSE....?
DO YOU THINK....?
WHAT IS YOUR OPINION OF....?
WHO SHOULD....?
WHAT MIGHT HAPPEN IF....?
DO YOU VALUE....?
IS IT MORAL TO....?

DON'T sell out important principles for money, a scholarship, a diploma, popularity, or a feeling of importance.

DON'T think you have to associate with morally corrupt people or sanction their corruption just because 'society' now accepts such behavior.

DON'T get discouraged. If you stick to firm principles, others will respect you for it, and perhaps gain courage from your example.

….And now some DO's for parents, teachers and students.

DO insist on quality in education.

DO have the courage to back up your convictions.

DO explain any objections you might have to textbooks, materials or instruction.

DO complain in writing (keep copy) to the highest level about courses that have no substance, which teach falsehood, force unsubstantiated theories and opinions, or indoctrinate in the Humanist and Humanitarian religions.
(College level – To trustees, or to board of regents and legislators if tax-supported.)
(High school & grade school – To school boards, administrators and legislators.)

DO send copies of important letters with documented complaints to the news media.

DO give specific examples of the most offensive sections of offensive materials to officials, school boards, etc. when you complain.

DO explain as clearly as possible how you want the situation to be corrected.

DO suggest better materials if you know of any, but do not take the burden of finding better materials on yourself. It is the duty of the educational institution to have good Constitutionally acceptable materials on hand.

DO stand up publicly for the teachers or administrators who insist on firm, fair discipline and quality education.

DO make your complaints as widely known as possible among other parents, teachers and students who are affected.

DO expect efforts to put you down, to distract you, and to discourage you by inaction.

DO persevere.

Of all acts of cowardice, the meanest is that which leads us to abandon a good cause because it is weak, and join a bad cause because it is strong.
James McCosh, D.D., L.L.D.

References

1. THE SCIENCE OF POWER, Benjamin Kidd, G.P. Putnam's Sons, N.Y., London, 1918, Page 309.

2. EDWARD BELLAMY, SELECTED WRITINGS ON RELIGION AND SOCIETY, Joseph Schiffman, Ed. Liberal Arts Press, New York, 23, N.Y. 1955, Page 18.

3. A SOCIOLOGICAL PHILOSOPHY OF EDUCATION, Ross L. Finney, Ph.D., MacMillan, 1928, Page 118.

4. THE POSITIVE PHILOSOPHY OF AGUSTE COMTE, Translated by Harriet Martineau, George Bell, London, 1896, Vo. III, Page 3.

5. Ibid., Vol II., Page 170.

6. ENCYCLOPEDIA BRITANNICA, "Auguste Comte", Volume 6, Page 191, Fourteenth Edition.

7. POSITIVISM IN THE UNITED STATES (1853-1861), Richmond Laurin Hawkins, Ph.D., Harvard University Press, 1938, Page 95.

8. A SOCIOLOGICAL PHILOSOPHY OF EDUCATION, page 145.

9. THE RECONSTRUCTION OF RELIGION, Charles A. Ellwood, Ph.D., Professor of Sociology, U. of Missouri, MacMillan Company, 1923, Page 177.

10. OUR CHANGING SOCIAL ORDER, Gavian, Gray, & Groves, D.C. Heath & Company, Boston, 1941, Page 17.

11. CHRISTIANITY AND SOCIAL SCIENCE, Charles A. Ellwood, Ph.D., MacMillan Company, 1923, Page 19.

12. A SOCIOLOGICAL PHILOSOPHY OF EDUCATION, Page 61.

13. "Tyranny of All the People," ARENA MAGAZINE, July, 1891, Rev. Francis Bellamy.

14. A SOCIOLOGICAL PHILOSOPHY OF EDUCAITON, Page 117.

15. Ibid. Page 56.

16. THE SCIENCE OF POWER, Page 124.

17. KNOWLEDGE PROCESSES AND VALUES IN THE NEW SOCIAL STUDIES, a handbook for teachers published by the Wisconsin Department of Public Instruction, Page 45.

18. A SOCIOLOGICAL PHILOSOPHY OF EDUCATION, Page 8.

19. THE PRINCIPLES OF SOCIOLOGY, Franklin Henry Giddings, M.A. MacMillan, 1896, Page 17.

20. THE SCIENCE OF POWER, Page 7.

21. A SOCIOLOGICAL PHILOSOPHY OF EDUCATION, Page 416.

22. THE SCIENCE OF POWER, Page 144.

23. Ibid. Page 236.

24. KNOWLEDGE PROCESSES AND VALUES, Page 43.

25. RECONSTRUCTION OF RELIGION, Page 203.

26. Ibid. Page 200.

Other References

HOLY BIBLE, King James Version

THE DIALOGUES OF PLATO, B. Jowett, M.A. Random House, New York.

OUR LIBERAL MOVEMENT IN THEOLOGY, Joseph Henry Allen, Roberts Brothers, Boston, 1882

SOCIAL CONTROL, Joseph S. Roucek, Ph.E. (Ed.), D. Van Nostrand Co., 1947.

AUGUSTE COMTE AND POSITIVISM, John Stewart Mill, Ann Arbor Paperbacks, University Michigan Press, 1961.

THE MAGIC OF NUMBERS, Eric Temple Bell, Whittlesey House, McGraw-Hill, New York-London, 1946.

LOOKING BACKWARD, Edward Bellamy, Random House, New York, 1951.

EQUALITY, Edward Bellamy, D. Appleton and Company, New York, 1951.

A CENTURY OF EDUCATION, J.M. Dent & Co., London, 1908.

THE WORLD'S PARLIAMENT OF RELIGIONS, Ed. by Rev. John Henry Barrows, D.D., The Parliament Publishing Company, Chicago, 1893.

SOCIOLOGY, Paul B. Horton, Chester L. Hunt, McGraw-Hill, 1964.

SOCIOLOGY AND SOCIAL LIFE, Raymond W. Mack, Kimball Young, American Book Company, 1968.

SOCIOLOGY FOR HIGH SCHOOL, Suzanne Harris Sandkowsky, Oxford Book Company, New York, N.Y., 1969.

SOCIOLOGY, Paul H. Landis, Ginn and Company, Boston, 1967.

SOCIOLOGY, ITS PURPOSE AND SCOPE, Harold J. Reddan, John J. Saal, William H. Sadlier, Inc., 1970.

VALUES AND TEACHING, Louis E. Raths, Merrill Marmin, Sidney B. Simon, Charles E. Merrill Publishing Co., Columbus, Ohio, 1966.